Spanish & English Comments for Report Cards & Notes Going Home

by Audrey Clifford Lang

Carson-Dellosa Publishing Company, Inc.
Greensboro, North Carolina

Credits

Project Director
Jennifer Weaver-Spencer

Translations
Translations.com

Layout Design
Jon Nawrocik

ISBN 0-88724-271-5

Contents

It is not always easy to encapsulate a child's performance within the guidelines of a report card, especially when the child's parents do not speak English. It can also be difficult to find the words (even in English!) to help parents understand where their child is, what their child's gifts are, and in what areas their child needs to improve.

Spanish & English Comments for Report Cards & Notes Going Home offers a variety of positive and constructive messages to help you inform and communicate with Spanish-speaking parents throughout the year. This book is a guide to help you communicate with Spanish-speaking parents through a student's report card and other correspondence.

While not intended as a comprehensive communication system, *Spanish & English Comments for Report Cards & Notes Going Home* will provide you with the basic tools needed to communicate with your students' Spanish-speaking parents. Whenever possible, use this book along with help from Spanish-speaking teachers or other bilingual school employees.

How to Use This Book:

- Use the contents on pages 3-4 to locate the appropriate section for the type of comment you wish to make. Then, determine which comment is appropriate for your situation.
- In Spanish, many words have gender. All Spanish nouns, including pronouns, are male or female. *Él* and *ella* mean he and she, and are also the masculine and feminine words for the. (*El* as an article does not have an accent.) For example, the masculine "He is intelligent/*Él es inteligente*," would become feminine "She is intelligent/*Ella es inteligente.*"
- Occasionally, a Spanish comment may also include an adjective that ends in *o* or *a*, and therefore changes gender with the noun it modifies. In these cases, masculine "Juan is studious/*Juan es estudioso*," becomes feminine "Juana is studious/*Juana es estudiosa.*"
- All Spanish comments note gender changes in articles and adjectives with parentheses, "*Es atento(a) y cortés en clase*," or slashes, "*Esto ha sido muy frustrante para él/ella.*" The masculine is always noted first and the feminine is always noted second.
- After making modifications for gender, write or type the comment in Spanish. Be careful to include all accents and special characters because they are important and necessary. Without appropriate accents, you may be using an entirely different word with an inappropriate meaning.
  - To create é, í, ó, and á on a Macintosh computer, type option e, then the appropriate letter. Type option n and then n to create ñ.
  - When typing comments on a PC, hold down the right ALT key, then type a letter to make a letter with the appropriate accent.
  - These accent marks also affect pronunciation. An accent over a vowel indicates that its syllable is stressed.
- In most Spanish-speaking countries, it is commonplace to use question marks or exclamation points both before and after questions or exclamations. The punctuation at the beginnings of sentences should be upside down.
  - To type ¿ on a Macintosh, hold down shift and option and type a question mark.
  - To type ¡ on a Macintosh, hold down option and type 1. To type an ¿ or a ¡ on a PC, hold down the right ALT key, then type the English character.

Features of This Book:

- **Spanish and English comments for report cards and notes going home** are located on pages 12-78. These comments be used when communicating with both Spanish- and English-speaking parents. A variety of positive and constructive comments are provided for various subject areas and other school-related topics. General Succeeding/Improving and Concerns, as well as Welcome Back and Beginning of the School Year messages, are also included. If parents can speak some English, you may choose to include both the Spanish and the English versions of the same comments in your notes.
- A **pronunciation guide** is located on page 7.
- On pages 8-10 is a **word bank** featuring words commonly used school and classroom words. These words are categorized by subject areas for easy reference.
- **Days of the week, months of the year, numbers 0-100, and ordinal numbers 1-12** are listed on pages 10-11.
- **Stationery and note templates** are included on pages 79-80. Because the words for teacher differ depending on a teacher's gender, male teachers should use the *Nota del Maestro* template, and female teachers should use the *Nota del Maestra* template. Both templates are on page 79.
- To help you track parent communications, a ***Parent Communication Log*** is included on page 80. Use this page to record dates of notes and other communications home, as well as important information about each student's family.

Spanish Pronunciation Guide

There are more letters in the Spanish alphabet than in the English alphabet. In Spanish there are 30: A, B, C, CH, D, E, F, G, H, I, J, K, L, LL, M, N, Ñ, O, P, Q, R, RR, S, T, U, V, W, X, Y, Z.

LETTER	SPANISH SOUND	ENGLISH SOUND	WORD
a	ah	h<u>o</u>t	a
b	b	<u>b</u>oat	be
c	k or s	<u>c</u>ut, <u>c</u>ity	ce (say)
ch	ch	<u>ch</u>urch	che
d	d	<u>d</u>ig	de
e	long a	<u>a</u>te	e
f	f	<u>f</u>oot	efe
g	g or h	<u>g</u>o or <u>h</u>ouse	ge
h	(silent)	(silent)	hache
i	ee	m<u>ee</u>t	i
j	breathy h	<u>h</u>at	jota
k	k	<u>k</u>ite	ka
l	l	<u>l</u>ittle	ele
ll	y	<u>y</u>am	elle
m	m	<u>m</u>ore	eme
n	n	<u>n</u>ice	ene
ñ	ny	on<u>i</u>on	eñe
o	o	c<u>oa</u>t	o
p	p	<u>p</u>ull	pe
q	ku	<u>c</u>ool	cu
r	r	<u>r</u>ule	ere
rr	trilled r	not in English	erre
s	s	<u>s</u>ew	ese
t	t	<u>t</u>ime	te
u	oo	c<u>oo</u>l	u
v	v or b	<u>v</u>ile or <u>b</u>oy	ve
w	w	<u>w</u>e	doble ve
x	ks	<u>x</u>ylophone	equis
y	y	<u>y</u>ellow	i griega
z	s	<u>s</u>uit	zeta

Basic Spanish Vocabulary
Vocabulario Español Básico

Language Arts
- Capitalization
- Grammar
- Handwriting
- Oral Communication
- Penmanship
- Punctuation
- Reading
- Spelling
- Writing

Artes del lenguaje
- Uso de mayúsculas
- Gramática
- Escritura
- Comunicación oral
- Caligrafía
- Puntuación
- Lectura
- Ortografía
- Composición

Math
- Addition
- Division
- Estimation
- Factoring
- Fractions
- Graphing
- Multiplication
- Place Value
- Subtraction
- Word Problems

Matemáticas
- Suma
- División
- Estimación
- Descomposición en factores
- Fracciones
- Gráficas
- Multiplicación
- Valor relativo
- Resta
- Problemas escritos

Science
- Alcohol
- Biology
- Chemistry
- Drugs
- Environment
- Experiments
- Food
- Food Pyramid
- Human Body
- Nutrition
- Simple Machines
- Sounds
- Taste
- Texture

Ciencias
- Alcohol
- Biología
- Drogas
- Química
- Medio ambiente
- Experimentos
- Alimentos
- Pirámide de los alimentos
- Cuerpo humano
- Nutrición
- Máquinas simples
- Sonidos
- Sabor
- Textura

Social Studies
Branches of government:
- Executive
- Legislative
- Judicial

Ciencias sociales
Ramas del gobierno:
- Ejecutiva
- Legislativa
- Judicial

- Capital
- Country
- Current Events
- Directions
- Economics
- Government
- History
- Map Skills
- Our State
- United States

Computer
- Internet
- Keyboard
- Programming
- Typing

Art and Music
- Charcoal
- Clay
- Drawing
- Instrument
- Music
- Painting
- Pen
- Pencil
- Scissors Skills
- Voice
- Watercolor

Physical Education
- Cooperative Play
- Coordination
- Gym
- Motor Skills
- Spatial Awareness
- Sportsmanship

School Supplies
- Backpack
- Book Bag
- Calculator
- Calendar
- Crayons
- Desk
- Graph Paper
- Homework
- Notebook
- Notebook Paper

- Capital
- País
- Sucesos de actualidad
- Instrucciones
- Economía
- Gobierno
- Historia
- Destrezas con mapas
- Nuestro Estado
- Estados Unidos

Computadora
- Internet
- Teclado
- Programación
- Mecanografía

Arte y música
- Carboncillo
- Barro
- Dibujo
- Instrumento
- Música
- Pintura
- Bolígrafo
- Lápiz
- Destrezas con las tijeras
- Voz
- Acuarela

Educación física
- Juego en cooperación
- Coordinación
- Gimnasio
- Habilidades motoras
- Conciencia espacial
- Espíritu deportivo

Útiles escolares
- Mochila
- Bolsa para libros
- Calculadora
- Calendario
- Crayones
- Escritorio
- Papel cuadriculado
- Tarea
- Cuaderno
- Papel para cuaderno

- Organizer
- Pen
- Pencil
- Ruler
- Textbook

People
- Counselor
- Resource Teacher
- Student
- Teacher
- Tutor
- Volunteer

Allergy Foods
- Nuts
- Dairy Products

School and School Grounds
- Cafeteria
- Hallway
- Library
- Media Center
- Playground

Days of the Week
- Monday
- Tuesday
- Wednesday
- Thursday
- Friday
- Saturday
- Sunday

Months of the Year
- January
- February
- March
- April
- May
- June
- July
- August
- September
- October
- November
- December

- Organizador
- Bolígrafo
- Lápiz
- Regla
- Libro de texto

Gente
- Consejero
- Maestro de materia
- Estudiante
- Maestro
- Tutor
- Voluntario

Comidas que causan alergias
- Nueces
- Productos lácteos

Escuela e instalaciones escolares
- Cafetería
- Pasillo
- Biblioteca
- Centro de medios de comunicación
- Patio de recreo

Los Días de la Semana
- lunes
- martes
- miércoles
- jueves
- viernes
- sábado
- domingo

Los Meses del Año
- enero
- febrero
- marzo
- abril
- mayo
- junio
- julio
- agosto
- septiembre
- octubre
- noviembre
- diciembre

Numbers 0-100/Numeros 0-100
Ordinal Numbers 1-12/Los Números Ordinales

NUMBERS 0-100

NUMEROS 0-100

0..... zero ....cero	39 .. thirty nine ...... treinta y nueve	81 ... eighty one .... ochenta y uno
1..... one .... uno	40... forty ....cuarenta	82... eighty two ....ochenta y dos
2..... two................................dos	41 ... forty one......... cuarenta y uno	83... eighty three ..... ochenta y trés
3..... three .... tres	42... forty two .... cuarenta y dos	84... eighty four... ochenta y cuatro
4..... four .... cuatro	43... forty three ...... cuarenta y trés	85... eighty five ...... ochenta y cinco
5..... five .... cinco	44... forty four........ cuarenta y séis	86... eighty six......... ochenta y séis
6..... six .... seis	45... forty five ......cuarenta y cinco	87....eighty seven ....ochenta y siete
7..... seven .... siete	46... forty six .... cuarenta y séis	88... eighty eight.....ochenta y ocho
8..... eight ....ocho	47... forty seven ....cuarenta y siete	89... eighty nine ... ochenta y nueve
9..... nine .... nueve	48... forty eight..... cuarenta y ocho	90... ninety .... noventa
10... ten............................... diez	49... forty nine.....cuarenta y nueve	91... ninety one ...... noventa y uno
11 ... eleven .... once	50... fifty......................... cincuenta	92... ninety two ....noventa y dos
12... twelve .... doce	51... fifty one ....cincienta y uno	93... nincty three ..... noventa y trés
13... thirteen........................trece	52... fifty two......... cincienta y dos	94... ninety four... noventa y cuatro
14... fourteen .... catorce	53... fifty three.......cincienta y trés	95... ninety five ...... noventa y cinco
15... fifteen .... quince	54... fifty four .....cincienta y cuatro	96... ninety six......... noventa y séis
16... sixteen..................... dieciséis	55... fifty five .... cincienta y cinco	97... ninety seven ... noventa y siete
17... seventeen .... diecisiete	56... fifty six ....cincienta y séis	98... ninety eight ....noventa y ocho
18... eighteen.................. dieciocho	57... fifty seven ..... cincienta y siete	99... ninety nine ... noventa y nueve
19... nineteen .... diecinueve	58... fifty eight ...... cincienta y ocho	100..one hundred.........cien (ciento)
20... twenty .... veinte	59... fifty nine ..... cincienta y nueve	
21... twenty one .... veintiuno	60... sixty .... sesenta	
22... twenty two .... veintidós	61... sixty one .... sesenta y uno	
23... twenty three .... veintitrés	62... sixty two .... sesenta y dos	
24... twenty four......... veinticuatro	63... sixty three .... sesenta y trés	
25... twenty five...........veinticinco	64... sixty four...... sesenta y cuatro	
26... twenty six .... veintiséis	65... sixty five.........sesenta y cinco	
27... twenty seven .... veintisiete	66... sixty six........... sesenta y séis	
28... twenty eight .... veintiocho	67... sixty seven ......sesenta y siete	
29... twenty nine .... veintinueve	68... sixty eight ...... sesenta y ocho	
30... thirty .... treinta	69... sixty nine ......sesenta y nueve	

ORDINAL NUMBERS 1-12

LOS NÚMEROS ORDINALES 1-12

31 ... thirty one .... treinta y uno	70... seventy .... setenta	first..................................... primero
32... thirty two ....treinta y dos	71... seventy one ...... setenta y uno	second...........................el segundo
33... thirty three .... treinta y trés	72... seventy two ....setenta y dos	third .... el tercero
34... thirty four...... treinta y cuatro	73... seventy three .... setenta y trés	fourth .... cuarto
35... thirty five........ treinta y cinco	74....seventy four... setenta y cuatro	fifth .... quinto
36... thirty six........... treinta y séis	75... seventy five.... setenta y cinco	sixth .... sexto
37... thirty seven ...... treinta y siete	76... seventy six .... setenta y séis	seventh................................ séptimo
38... thirty eight ....treinta y ocho	77... seventy seven .. setenta y siete	eighth .... octavo
	78... seventy eight ...setenta y ocho	ninth .... noveno
	79....seventy nine.... setenta y nueve	tenth.................................. décimo
	80... eighty .... ochenta	eleventh......................... undécimo
		twelfth......................... duodécimo

General Comments
Comentarios Generales

General Succeeding/Improving

_____ is succeeding in _____ . I am pleased with her excellent work.

_____ is a great student. He is doing very well in _____ this year.

_____ has improved in _____ . She should be proud of her progress.

_____ 's work in _____ has shown improvement. I am happy with his recent success in _____ .

General Concerns

_____ is having trouble in _____ . Please encourage her to try her hardest in this area.

_____ is struggling with work in _____ class. I believe that with extra effort, she will become successful in _____ .

In order to help _____ progress more quickly, I will be sending home extra work for _____ to complete in _____ .

Welcome Back Messages

Hello, my name is _____ , and I will be your _____ grade teacher this fall. Our class will meet in room _____ . There will be _____ other students in our class. I know we will all have a great year together. See you on _____ .

Logros en general/Mejoría

_____ va muy bien en _____ . Estoy satisfecho(a) con su excelente trabajo.

_____ es un(a) buen(a) estudiante. Va muy bien en _____ este año.

_____ ha mejorado en _____ . Debe estar orgulloso(a) de su progreso.

El trabajo de _____ en _____ ha mejorado. Estoy contento(a) con su reciente logro en _____ .

Preocupaciones generales

_____ tiene problema en _____ . Por favor, anímelo(a) a esforzarse más en esta área.

_____ tiene dificultades en _____ . Yo creo que con un poco más de esfuerzo tendrá éxito en _____ .

Para ayudarle a _____ a progresar más rápidamente, voy a darle tarea adicional para que _____ la complete en _____ .

Mensajes de bienvenida de regreso a clases

Hola, me llamo _____ , y seré tu maestro(a) de _____ año. Nuestra clase se reunirá en el salón _____ . Habrá _____ estudiantes en nuestra clase. Sé que tendremos un buen año escolar juntos. Nos vemos el _____ .

Congratulations! You're going to be in the _____ grade! Some of the things we will be learning about are _____ . I look forward to having you in my class.

The start of the new school year is almost here. I am looking forward to meeting you. When you come to school, go to room _____ . Please bring the following items with you: a pencil, a notebook and paper, one of your favorite stories, something you would like to share with your classmates, and one thing you would like to learn about.

Welcome to the _____ grade! My name is _____ , and I will be your new teacher. I am very excited about the upcoming year. We will be exploring new topics and learning many new things. I am looking forward to meeting you.

¡Felicitaciones! Vas a estar en _____ grado. Algunas de las cosas que vamos a aprender son _____ . Me da gusto tenerte en mi clase.

El comienzo del año escolar ya casi está aquí. Espero conocerte pronto. Cuando vengas a la escuela, ve al salón _____ . Por favor, trae lo siguiente: lápiz, cuaderno, papel, uno de tus cuentos favoritos, algo que quieras compartir con tus compañeros de clase y alguna cosa de la cual te gustaría aprender algo.

¡Bienvenido al _____ grado! Me llamo _____ , y voy a ser tu nuevo(a) maestro(a). Estoy muy entusiasmado(a) por este nuevo año. Vamos a explorar nuevos temas y aprender muchas cosas nuevas. Espero conocerte pronto.

Beginning of the School Year
Adjusting Well
You should be very proud of _____ . This has been a busy time, with everyone getting to know each other and adjusting to new schedules. She has been doing very well and seems to be comfortable and happy in class.

I just wanted you to know that _____ follows directions in class. He has adapted to the routine and actively participates in class. He seems eager to share his ideas and puts forth a lot of effort in class.

Inicio del año escolar
Buena adaptación
Usted debe estar muy orgulloso(a) de _____ Este ha sido un periodo de mucha actividad, todos están empezando a conocerse y a adaptarse a nuevos horarios. Él/Ella va muy bien y parece estar cómodo(a) y contento(a) en clase.

Sólo quería que usted supiera que _____ obedece las instrucciones que se dan en clase. Se ha adaptado a la rutina y participa activamente en clase. Parece dispuesto(a) a compartir sus ideas y pone mucho esfuerzo en clase.

I am enjoying getting to know _____ . She is a very good student, and I can always count on her to help her classmates. I am pleased to have _____ as part of my class.

Estoy disfrutando conocer a _____ . Es buen(a) estudiante y siempre puedo contar con él/ella para ayudar a sus compañeros. Me da gusto tener a _____ en nuestra clase.

_____ is off to a wonderful start. We have been reviewing last year's material, and he has a good grasp of the concepts. He comes to school prepared and ready to work.

_____ ha comenzado muy bien. Hemos estado revisando material del año pasado y ha comprendido bien los conceptos. Viene a clase preparado(a) y listo(a) para trabajar.

_____ is a pleasure to have in class. She has settled into her new schedule and has adjusted nicely to the new surroundings and routine. She is attentive and courteous in class.

Es un placer tener a _____ en clase. Se ha acostumbrado a su nuevo horario y se ha adaptado bien a su nuevo ambiente y rutina. Es atento(a) y cortés en clase.

It is a delight to have _____ in class. Although he tends to be quiet, he does not hesitate to try new things. He is eager to participate, takes suggestions well, and puts forth excellent effort.

Es bueno tener a _____ en clase. Aunque es callado(a), no duda en probar cosas nuevas. Está dispuesto(a) a participar, toma sugerencias de buena manera y trabaja con muchas ganas.

Difficulty Adjusting

The school year began well, and _____ seemed to be adjusting. Recently, however, he has been having behavior problems in class. I am a concerned and would appreciate it if you would discuss the situation with him.

Dificultad para adaptarse

El año escolar comenzó bien, y _____ parecía estar adaptándose. Sin embargo, recientemente ha tenido problemas de comportamiento en clase. Me preocupa esto y apreciaría que usted hablara de esta situación con él/ella.

_____ seldom joins in with her classmates and seems to prefer to be alone. I am encouraging her to work and play with a few students with whom she seems most comfortable and expect the situation will improve with time.

_____ raramente se junta con sus compañeros y prefiere estar solo(a). Lo/La estoy animando a trabajar y jugar con estudiantes con quienes parece estar más cómodo(a). Espero que la situación mejore con el tiempo.

School has been in session for a few weeks, and I am concerned that _____ seems to be having difficulty getting organized. She forgets to bring her materials to school and often cannot find her _____ . Perhaps a book bag, backpack, or tote bag would help _____ keep her school things together.

Although it is early in the year, it is apparent that _____ is having some trouble with _____ . Since extra help and support may be needed in this area, I would like to have _____ work with him a few times a week.

La escuela ya tiene algunas semanas de haber comenzado y me preocupa que _____ parece tener dificultad para organizarse. Olvida traer sus útiles a la escuela y con frecuencia no puede encontrar su _____ . Quizá una mochila o bolsa para libros pueda ayudar a _____ a mantener juntas sus cosas de la escuela.

Aunque todavía es muy pronto en el año, es evidente que _____ tiene cierta dificultad con _____ . Dado que es posible que se necesite apoyo adicional en esta área, me gustaría que _____ trabajara con él/ella algunas veces por semana.

Language Arts
Artes del lenguaje

Reading
Succeeding/Improving

I am very pleased to tell you that _____ knows all of the sounds of the alphabet and is very good at sounding out words. These skills will help him become a strong reader.

I am very pleased with_____ 's progress. He easily recognizes the basic sight words and can use them in sentences.

_____ is a fluent reader. She enjoys reading on her own and participating in book discussions.

Lectura
Logros/Mejoría

Me complace informarle que _____ sabe todos los sonidos del alfabeto y es muy bueno(a) para sacar los sonidos de las palabras. Estas habilidades le ayudarán a convertirse en un buen lector.

Estoy muy satisfecho(a) con el progreso de _____ . Fácilmente reconoce de vista las palabras básicas y puede usarlas en frases completas.

_____ lee con fluidez. Disfruta de leer por su propia cuenta y de participar en conversaciones sobre libros.

Struggling

_____ does not immediately recognize all of the basic sight words but is working hard to learn them. _____ has made a personal set of sight word flash cards to work with every day. He will be bringing them home to practice.

I feel that _____ would benefit from reading more outside of school. I have included a list of some books you can check out from the public library. Please encourage _____ to read these books on his own or to you.

Avance con dificultad

_____ no reconoce de vista todas las palabras básicas inmediatamente, pero está trabajando mucho para aprenderlas. _____ ha hecho un juego personal de tarjetas con estas palabras para practicarlas diariamente. Las va a llevar a casa para practicar.

Siento que a _____ le beneficiaría leer más fuera de la escuela. He incluido una lista de libros que usted puede sacar de la biblioteca local.

I am a concerned because _____ does not seem to retain enough of what he reads. Many times he has to reread a story or passage before answering questions. I believe that the more he reads the better his comprehension skills will become. It would be very helpful if you could encourage _____ to read for twenty minutes every night and then tell you about what he has read.

Me preocupa que _____ no parece retener mucho de lo que lee. Muchas veces tiene que releer un cuento o un pasaje antes de contestar preguntas. Creo que entre más lea, su comprensión de lectura mejorará. Sería bueno que usted animara a _____ a leer por veinte minutos cada noche y que luego le diga lo que ha leído.

_____ reads at a slow pace and does not seem to enjoy reading. I plan to send home materials that I feel will interest her. It is my hope that _____ 's reading speed and enjoyment will increase the more she reads.

_____ lee despacio y no parece disfrutar de la lectura. Planeo enviar a su casa material que creo que le interesará. Espero que la velocidad de lectura de _____ mejore, así como su gusto por leer.

I am pleased that _____ loves books and reading. Although it may be just a matter of time before he is reading on grade level, right now he is struggling. Please encourage him to keep reading as much as possible and to make sure he does not become frustrated trying to read books that are too difficult.

Me da gusto que _____ disfrute de los libros y la lectura. Aunque puede ser sólo cuestión de tiempo antes de que él/ella esté al nivel de lectura de su grado escolar, ahora tiene dificultades. Por favor, anímelo(a) a seguir leyendo lo más posible y asegúrese de que no se frustre tratando de leer libros que sean muy difíciles.

Writing

_____ 's written work and overall effort have been good this past grading period. He took his assignments seriously and worked conscientiously. His last writing piece was excellent.

Composición

Las composiciones de _____ y su esfuerzo en general han sido buenos durante este último periodo escolar. Se tomó en serio sus asignaturas y trabajó concienzudamente. Su última composición fue excelente.

_____ enjoys writing and has a wonderful command of her spelling and vocabulary words. I am pleased with her progress.

_____ disfruta de escribir y tiene muy buen control de la ortografía y el vocabulario. Estoy satisfecho(a) con su progreso.

_____ has excellent writing skills. He clearly understands that every paragraph or story must have a beginning, middle, and end and writes accordingly. I want you to know how pleased I am with his progress.

_____ posee excelentes habilidades para escribir. Entiende claramente que cada párrafo o cuento tiene un comienzo, una parte media y un final, y escribe de acuerdo con esto. Quiero que sepa cuánto me complace su progreso.

_____ is having a hard time writing paragraphs. We will be doing more activities in class that I believe will help her develop better paragraph writing skills.

_____ does not seem to be enjoying our writers' workshop. She is having a difficult time putting her wonderful story ideas into words. It might help if you would encourage her to tell stories at home in English or in Spanish.

_____ is having a hard time putting his thoughts on paper. I will be encouraging him to do extra journal writing activities in order to help him in class. You may want to get _____ a notebook and encourage him to write in it at home.

_____ needs to develop better descriptive writing skills. Although _____ really enjoys writing, she has a difficult time including descriptive words. I will be encouraging _____ to reread her stories and to go back and add descriptive words. Perhaps when reading together in English or in Spanish at home you could discuss how the author describes a character or scene.

_____ needs help with book reports. I believe it would be very helpful if you would talk with _____ about each book she reads. Let her tell you the story and talk about her favorite parts before she starts writing her book report. I think this will help her better organize her thoughts.

We have been working on letter writing activities this week. We will be moving on to another topic next week, but _____ still needs more practice. It would be helpful if you could give him the names and addresses of people to whom he could write letters.

_____ tiene dificultades para escribir párrafos. Vamos a hacer más actividades en clase que creo le ayudarán a mejorar sus habilidades para escribir párrafos.

_____ no parece estar disfrutando nuestro taller de escritura. Le cuesta trabajo poner en palabras sus maravillosas ideas para escribir cuentos. Sería útil que usted lo/la animara a contar historias en casa, ya sea en inglés o en español.

A _____ le está costando trabajo poner sus pensamientos en el papel. Lo/La voy a animar a escribir un diario adicionalmente para ayudarle en clase. Quizá pueda usted conseguirle un cuaderno a _____ y animarlo(a) a escribir en él en casa.

_____ necesita desarrollar más su capacidad de descripción escrita. Aunque _____ realmente disfruta de escribir, le cuesta trabajo incluir palabras descriptivas. Voy a animar a _____ a releer sus historias para agregarles palabras descriptivas. Quizá cuando lea en casa, en inglés o en español, usted podría hablarle acerca de cómo el autor describe un personaje o una escena.

_____ necesita ayuda con sus informes sobre libros. Creo que sería útil que usted hablara con _____ sobre cada libro que lea. Deje que le cuente la historia y que hable de sus partes favoritas antes de empezar a escribir su reporte. Creo que esto le ayudaría a organizar mejor sus ideas antes de escribir.

Esta semana hemos estado trabajando en escribir cartas. Vamos a pasar a otros temas la próxima semana, pero _____ todavía necesita más práctica. Ayudaría que usted le diera nombres y direcciones de personas a quienes les pueda escribir.

Oral Communication Skills

_____ has a difficult time expressing himself verbally. It might help if you could encourage him to talk about his day and how he feels about school.

_____ is a very good reader, but she needs to practice reading aloud. Please encourage her to practice reading aloud to you at home. It would also be helpful for you to read aloud to her in English or in Spanish.

_____ is having a difficult time talking in front of a group or giving an oral presentation. We will be working on developing public speaking skills in class over the next few months. It might be helpful if you could let him practice reading out loud in front of you or your family.

Spelling

_____ is doing very well on her weekly spelling words and spelling assignments. Please encourage her to keep up the good work.

_____ has a great imagination and loves writing stories but needs to work on his spelling and grammar skills. I have given him a set of activity sheets to work on both in school and at home, which I believe will help him in these areas.

_____ would benefit from spending more time reviewing spelling words. A quick review each evening may be all that is required to see an improvement.

Destrezas de comunicación oral

A _____ le cuesta trabajo expresarse verbalmente. Podría ayudarle que usted lo/la alentara a que le cuente sobre cómo le fue en el día y cómo se siente en la escuela.

_____ es muy bueno(a) para leer, pero necesita practicar la lectura en voz alta. Por favor, anímelo(a) a leer en voz alta en casa. Sería bueno que usted le leyera en voz alta en inglés o español.

_____ tiene dificultades para hablar frente a la clase o dar una presentación oral. En clase, trabajaremos en el desarrollo de las destrezas para hablar en público durante los próximos meses. Podría ayudarle que lo/la dejara practicar la lectura en voz alta frente a usted o su familia.

Ortografía

_____ va muy bien en sus trabajos semanales de ortografía de palabras. Por favor, anímelo(a) a seguir haciendo un buen trabajo.

_____ tiene gran imaginación y le encanta escribir cuentos, pero necesita mejorar su ortografía y su gramática. Le he dado unas hojas con un juego de actividades para que practique tanto en la escuela como en su casa. Pienso que eso le ayudará en estas áreas.

A _____ le beneficiaría pasar más tiempo revisando su ortografía. Es posible que un breve repaso en la noche sea todo lo que necesite para mejorar.

_____ is having some difficulty with spelling. _____ will be making her own personal dictionary for her most frequently misspelled words. Please encourage her to use this dictionary when completing homework assignments.

_____ tiene dificultades con la ortografía. _____ va a hacer su propio diccionario con las palabras que más frecuentemente le salen mal. Por favor, motívelo(a) a usar este diccionario cuando haga su tarea.

Penmanship/Handwriting

_____ has wonderful handwriting for her age. It is a delight to read her work. Please encourage her to keep up the good work!

_____ needs to spend more time practicing his handwriting. It might help if he practiced at home by writing his own story or copying a favorite storybook or an article from the newspaper or a magazine.

Handwriting seems to be a real challenge for _____ . She is working on tracing letters in class and will be completing homework that should improve her skills.

Caligrafía/Escritura a mano

_____ tiene muy buena letra para su edad. Es un placer leer su trabajo. Por favor, anímelo(a) a seguir haciendo un buen trabajo.

_____ necesita pasar más tiempo practicando su escritura. Podría ayudarle practicar en casa escribiendo su propio cuento o copiando su cuento favorito o un artículo del periódico o de una revista.

Escribir a mano parece ser un verdadero reto para _____ . Está practicando el trazado de letras en clase y va a hacer tarea que le ayudará a mejorar.

Other

_____ loves reading, writing, and sharing her ideas. Her overall effort and participation have been excellent.

_____ is having a difficult time _____ . I will be sending home some extra worksheets for her to do over the next few weeks, which should help.

Otros

A _____ le encanta leer, escribir y compartir sus ideas. Su esfuerzo y participación han sido excelentes.

_____ tiene dificultades con _____ . Le voy a mandar a casa algunas hojas de trabajo adicionales para que las haga durante las próximas semanas, lo cual deberá ayudarle.

Math
Matemáticas

Succeeding/Improving

_____ is progressing nicely in math and is working on grade level. I am pleased with her progress.

_____ is an outstanding student in math. She grasps all of the concepts and seems to easily learn math processes.

Math is _____ 's best subject. He is doing well and working on grade level.

_____ 's success in math this year has been a very positive experience for her and has really helped build her self-confidence.

_____ is doing well in math. Please encourage him to continue to work hard.

_____ has made excellent progress and should be proud of how far she has come in math this year.

_____ should be very proud of himself. He has made a conscious effort to improve his math skills. Although progress has been slow, he has not given up. We need to continue to provide encouragement, both at school and at home.

_____ has improved dramatically in math. You should be proud of her progress.

Logros/Mejoría

_____ está avanzando bien en matemáticas y trabajando al nivel de su grado escolar. Estoy satisfecho(a) con su progreso.

_____ es un(a) estudiante excepcional en matemáticas. Entiende todos los conceptos y aprende fácilmente los procesos matemáticos.

Matemáticas es la mejor asignatura de _____ . Va bien y trabaja al nivel de su grado escolar.

El éxito que _____ ha tenido en matemáticas este año ha sido una experiencia muy positiva para él/ella y realmente le ha ayudado a mejorar su autoestima.

_____ va bien en matemáticas. Por favor, motívelo(a) a seguir trabajando mucho.

_____ ha logrado un excelente progreso y debe estar orgulloso(a) de lo mucho que ha logrado en matemáticas este año.

_____ debe sentirse muy orgulloso(a) de sí mismo(a). Ha hecho un esfuerzo consciente por mejorar sus habilidades matemáticas. Aunque el proceso ha sido lento, no se ha dado por vencido(a). Necesitamos seguir dándole ánimo, tanto en la escuela como en la casa.

_____ ha mejorado muchísimo en matemáticas. Debe estar orgulloso(a) de su progreso.

Needs Practice

_____ has a hard time grasping new math concepts. It would be helpful if you could encourage him to discuss the day's math activities at home in Spanish or in English. If he explains and reviews the day's concepts with you at home, it will help him better understand the concepts.

_____ is struggling with math. He is having a hard time applying the concepts he has learned to solve the problems we are doing. I believe he just needs extra practice. I am sending home some extra work that I think will help.

_____ 's strength seems to be memorizing the basic math facts. In order to help her become more successful in higher-level math skills, you may want to encourage her to do some fun logic and word problems books, available in the children's section at most book stores.

_____ needs to spend time at home reviewing what we have done in class. She is having a hard time with the concept of _____ . I believe that if she completes extra review time at home she will grasp the concept.

_____ is presenting _____ with her hardest math challenge this year. I will be sending extra work home with her, and it would really help if you would encourage her.

_____ seems to be a challenge for _____ . Although he is having a hard time with it now, I think with a little practice he will master it.

Necesita práctica

_____ tiene dificultades para comprender nuevos conceptos matemáticos. Sería beneficioso que usted lo/la animara a hablar sobre las actividades de matemáticas del día en casa, en español o en inglés. Si le explica y revisa los conceptos del día en casa, le ayudaría a entender mejor estos conceptos.

_____ está batallando con matemáticas. Tiene dificultades para aplicar los conceptos que ha aprendido para resolver los problemas que estemos haciendo. Creo que necesita practicar más. Le mandaré trabajo adicional que creo le ayudará.

La facilidad de _____ radica en memorizar datos básicos de matemáticas. Para ayudarlo(a) a mejorar sus habilidades en matemáticas de más alto nivel, quizá usted podría animarlo(a) a hacer juegos de lógica y problemas escritos de libros disponibles en la sección infantil de la mayoría de las librerías.

_____ necesita pasar tiempo en casa revisando lo que hemos hecho en clase. Tiene dificultades con el concepto de _____ . Creo que si dedica más tiempo a repasar en casa comprenderá estos conceptos.

_____ es el reto matemático más difícil del año para _____ . Voy a enviarle trabajo extra y ayudaría que usted le diera ánimos.

_____ parece ser un reto para _____ . Aunque tiene dificultad con esto ahora, creo que con un poco de práctica lo dominará.

_____ does not seem to grasp _____ . I will be sending additional work home with her.

_____ has not learned _____ , so her answers are often wrong. It would be helpful to _____ if you could work with her to practice _____ .

I am very pleased with _____ 's written math work. He has a difficult time communicating his work orally. He clearly knows which concepts or rules to apply, but he is unable to verbalize the information. It would be helpful if he could spend time telling you what we are doing in math. If he speaks only in general terms, ask if he could explain it to you by walking you through a problem we did in class. I believe _____ will benefit by discussing math in a situation where he is more comfortable.

_____ parece no entender _____ . Voy a enviarle trabajo adicional a casa.

_____ no ha aprendido _____ , por eso sus respuestas frecuentemente están mal. Sería beneficioso para _____ que usted pudiera trabajar con él/ella para practicar _____ .

Estoy muy contento(a) con el trabajo escrito de matemáticas de _____ . Tiene dificultades para comunicar su trabajo oralmente. Sabe claramente cuáles conceptos o reglas son aplicables, pero no puede verbalizarlo. Sería bueno que pasara un tiempo contándole lo que estamos haciendo en matemáticas. Si sólo habla en términos generales, pídale que le explique paso a paso el problema que hayamos hecho en clase. Creo que _____ se beneficiará hablando de matemáticas en una situación donde se encuentre más cómodo(a).

Struggling

Math is not _____ 's favorite subject, and it seems she is having a hard time concentrating and staying on task during math. Please encourage her to put forth her best effort during math class.

_____ does well with higher-level problem solving skills but cannot seem to master the basic facts. She needs to practice these facts at home. I will send home extra practice work for her to complete.

_____ is struggling to keep up and stay on grade level. I think he would benefit from doing extra work at home. I will send home some extra work.

Avance con dificultades

Matemáticas no es la materia favorita de _____ , y parece que tiene dificultades para concentrarse y seguir hasta el final un trabajo de matemáticas. Anímelo(a) a esforzarse en esta clase.

_____ resuelve bien problemas de un nivel más alto, pero no puede comprender la información básica. Necesita practicar más en casa, le enviaré tarea adicional.

_____ está batallando para mantenerse al nivel de su grado escolar. Creo que sería bueno que hiciera trabajo adicional en casa. Se lo enviaré.

_____ has mastered the basic facts but is having a difficult time tackling more complex concepts. She needs to remember to break the more difficult problems into smaller steps, instead of trying to complete them as a whole.

_____ does not seem to be putting forth his best effort when it comes to math. I really feel he could do better in math and think that if we encourage him both in school and at home his work will improve.

I am concerned that if _____ does not apply herself she will be left behind in math. We are moving on to _____ soon, and _____ is not ready. I will send home extra math work to help her catch up.

Attitude

_____ has a good attitude toward math but is progressing slowly and needs to practice _____ in order to keep up with his class work.

_____ 's attitude toward math needs improvement. Perhaps you could take advantage of opportunities at home to point out how math is used every day.

_____ feels that she is not good at math and is not putting forth an effort to improve her work. Please encourage her to do her best work.

_____ ha comprendido la información básica, pero tiene dificultades cuando se trata de conceptos más complejos. Necesita recordar que debe descomponer en partes el problema, en vez de tratar de hacerlo en un solo paso.

_____ no parece esforzarse mucho cuando se trata de matemáticas. Realmente, creo que podría ir mejor y pienso que si lo/la animamos, tanto en casa como en la escuela, su desempeño mejorará.

Me preocupa que si _____ no trabaja más, se va a retrasar en matemáticas. Vamos a pasar a _____ pronto, y _____ no está listo(a). Voy a enviarle trabajo adicional de matemáticas a casa para que se ponga al corriente.

Actitud

_____ tiene una buena actitud hacia las matemáticas, pero progresa lentamente y necesita practicar _____ para mantenerse al corriente con el trabajo de la clase.

La actitud de _____ hacia las matemáticas necesita mejorar. Quizá usted pueda aprovechar ciertas oportunidades en el hogar para señalarle cómo se usan las matemáticas cotidianamente.

_____ cree que no es bueno(a) en matemáticas y no se esfuerza para mejorar su trabajo. Por favor, ayúdelo(a) a mejorar su trabajo.

Careless Work

_____ needs to work on her neatness. Her math problems are often done wrong simply because she is not writing her work properly. I suggest that she complete her math work on graph paper to help her organize the problems.

_____ understands math concepts and knows what to do, but he is careless, so his answers are often incorrect. If he works more slowly and carefully, I believe his accuracy will improve.

_____ has excellent computation skills but her accuracy suffers because she does not check her work.

Trabajo descuidado

_____ necesita mejorar su pulcritud. Sus problemas matemáticos a menudo están mal simplemente porque no los escribió apropiadamente. Sugiero que haga su trabajo de matemáticas en papel cuadriculado para que pueda organizar los problemas.

_____ entiende conceptos matemáticos y sabe qué hacer, pero se descuida y sus respuestas están equivocadas con frecuencia. Si trabajara más despacio y con más cuidado, creo que su exactitud mejoraría.

_____ tiene excelentes habilidades para hacer cálculos, pero su exactitud no es tan buena porque no verifica su trabajo.

Science
Ciencias

Succeeding/Improving

I was pleased with _____ 's overall approach and achievements in science this grading period. She stayed focused during class and lab activities and consistently strove to do her best.

_____ 's homework assignments and lab reports exhibited a conscientious effort and showed a grasp of the material.

Although _____ often works too quickly and is at times impatient during science experiments, overall he demonstrates a good command of the concepts and facts that we covered this grading period.

_____ seems to enjoy science. She is always willing to participate and to help with experiments. She works well with others in a lab setting. I am very pleased to have her in my science class.

It is a pleasure having _____ in science class. I want to encourage him continue to pursue his science interests outside the classroom.

_____ seems to enjoy discovering the mysteries of science. She has an inquisitive mind. It is a pleasure to have her in science class.

Logros/Mejoría

Estuve contento(a) con la actitud en general y los logros de _____ en ciencias durante este periodo escolar. No perdió la concentración durante la clase ni en las actividades de laboratorio y siempre trató de hacer su trabajo lo mejor posible.

Las tareas y los reportes de laboratorio de _____ y mostraron esfuerzo consciente y comprensión del material.

A pesar de que _____ a veces trabaja muy rápidamente y en ocasiones se impacienta durante los experimentos de ciencias, demuestra buen dominio de los conceptos y la información que hemos visto durante este periodo escolar.

_____ parece disfrutar de la clase de ciencias. Siempre está dispuesto(a) a participar y a ayudar en los experimentos. Trabaja bien con los demás en un ambiente de laboratorio. Me complace tenerlo(a) en mi clase de ciencias.

Es un placer tener a _____ en la clase de ciencias. Quiero animarlo(a) a seguir su interés por las ciencias fuera del salón de clases.

_____ disfruta descubrir misterios de la ciencia. Tiene una mente inquisitiva. Es un placer tenerlo(a) en la clase de ciencias.

_____ has great leadership skills. He seems to naturally take the lead in many labs, and he is a positive influence. He makes sure all members participate and tries to make them feel that they are a part of the group. _____ is a natural leader and an excellent science student.

I know that science class has been a real challenge for _____ this year, with written work, lab work, research, and readings. I believe, however, that it has been a positive experience for her and should help her succeed in future studies.

I am very proud of _____ 's efforts to improve his science grade. Please encourage him to keep up the good work.

Struggling

_____ needs to work on her observation skills. She has trouble deciding what parts of the things she sees are important and should be recorded in her data book. Perhaps you could sprout a lima bean or another plant at home and _____ could practice recording daily observations in her data book.

_____ is having a difficult time verbalizing her thoughts and observations in science. She does a wonderful job writing them but has a hard time sharing them aloud. We will be spending more time on oral presentations in class. I believe with time and practice, _____ 's oral presentation skills will improve. Perhaps she could practice at home by telling you about what she has been observing and doing in science class.

_____ tiene grandes dotes de líder. Asume el liderazgo con naturalidad en muchos experimentos de laboratorio y es una influencia positiva. Se asegura de que todos participen y trata de hacerlos sentir parte del grupo. _____ es un(a) líder nato(a) y un(a) estudiante sobresaliente de ciencias.

Sé que la clase de ciencias ha sido un reto para _____ este año, con el trabajo escrito, laboratorio, investigación y lecturas. Sin embargo, creo que la experiencia ha sido positiva y le ayudará a tener éxito en sus estudios futuros.

Estoy muy orgulloso(a) del esfuerzo de _____ para mejorar sus calificaciones en la clase de ciencias. Por favor, motívelo(a) a seguir haciendo un buen trabajo.

Avance con dificultades

_____ necesita mejorar su capacidad de observación. Tiene problemas para decidir qué partes de lo que ve son importantes y deben registrarse en su libro de datos. Quizá usted pueda poner a germinar un frijol u otra planta en casa y _____ podría practicar registrando sus observaciones diarias en su libro de datos.

A _____ le cuesta trabajo verbalizar sus pensamientos y observaciones científicas. Las escribe bien, pero le cuesta trabajo compartirlas en voz alta. Vamos a pasar más tiempo en presentaciones orales en clase. Creo que con tiempo y práctica, _____ mejorará sus presentaciones orales. Quizá podría practicar en casa contándole a usted lo que ha observado y hecho en la clase de ciencias.

I am concerned because _____ has missed several science assignments. She cannot continue to miss assignments and do well in class. I will be sending home a list of the assignments and their due dates. If possible, please help her turn in all work on time.

_____ has a positive attitude toward science and clearly gives his best effort, although he is struggling to keep up. He will need our help and support. I will be sending home some extra activities that I think will help.

Attitude and Behavior

_____ is an active participant in class when she can refer to her prepared assignments but not when we discuss new material. _____ is very good in science. I would like to see her get more involved in discussions that initiate new topics.

_____ is very unsure of himself in science class and is hesitant to participate in experiments. In order to help build his self-confidence, I will give him some simple experiments to do at home. It would help _____ succeed if you would make sure he completes each experiment and records all observations in his lab book.

I am concerned because _____ does not always practice safety in science class. She consistently needs to be reminded to _____ . I hope that you will help me convince _____ of the importance of safety in the lab.

Me preocupa que _____ no ha hecho varias tareas de ciencias. No puede seguir sin hacer estos trabajos y salir bien en clase. Le enviaré una lista de las tareas y sus fechas de entrega. Si fuera posible, ayúdelo(a) a entregar a tiempo sus trabajos.

_____ tiene buena actitud hacia la ciencia y claramente trabaja mucho, aunque está luchando para mantenerse al corriente. Va a necesitar nuestra ayuda y apoyo. Enviaré actividades adicionales a casa que pienso le ayudarán.

Actitud y comportamiento

_____ es un(a) participante activo(a) en clase cuando se puede referir a su tarea, pero no cuando presentamos material nuevo. _____ es muy bueno(a) en ciencias. Me gustaría que participara más en discusiones sobre nuevos temas.

_____ se siente muy inseguro(a) en la clase de ciencias y duda en participar en los experimentos. Para ayudarle a mejorar su autoestima, le daré algunos experimentos sencillos para que los haga en casa. A _____ le ayudaría que usted se asegurara de que complete cada experimento y registre todas sus observaciones en su libro de laboratorio.

Me preocupa que _____ no siempre practica medidas de seguridad en la clase de ciencias. Con frecuencia, es necesario recordarle _____ . Espero que usted me ayude a convencer a _____ de la importancia de ser precavido(a) en el laboratorio.

_____ enjoys participating in science experiments and has a good understanding of the concepts we are studying. I am concerned that she tends to play with the materials in the lab. I have explained to her that this can be very dangerous and that she must take more care if she wants to continue to participate.

_____ does not seem to like science. I believe she will need encouragement, both at school and at home, in order to be successful. Please take opportunities as to explain how science is used in our lives.

_____ disfruta participar en experimentos científicos y tiene buena comprensión de los conceptos que estamos estudiando. Me preocupa que tiende a jugar con los materiales del laboratorio. Le he explicado que esto puede ser muy peligroso y que debe tener más cuidado si quiere seguir participando.

A _____ parecen no agradarle las ciencias. Creo que necesitará motivación, tanto en la escuela como en casa, para tener éxito. Por favor, aproveche las oportunidades que tenga para explicarle cómo se usa la ciencia en nuestras vidas.

Informing Parents of Class Activities

We will be completing science experiments on texture and taste soon. The class will be eating a variety of foods and recording their impressions of each. If _____ has any food allergies, please fill out and return the enclosed form. You could help _____ with this project if you would discuss the foods you eat at dinner and let him try to express what their textures and tastes are like.

We have been studying food and nutrition. I have asked each student to keep a diary of all of the foods she eats and to categorize the foods into the basic food groups. If possible, discuss what foods you eat at dinner and in what groups they belong. This would help _____ gain a better understanding.

Informando a los padres de familia de las actividades de la clase

Muy pronto, vamos a hacer experimentos científicos sobre textura y sabor. Los estudiantes van a comer varios alimentos y a registrar sus impresiones de cada uno. Si _____ tiene alguna alergia alimenticia, llene y devuelva la forma anexa. Usted ayudaría a _____ con este proyecto, si hablara sobre los alimentos que ustedes comen y dejara que él/ella exprese cómo son los sabores y texturas.

Hemos estado estudiando alimentos y nutrición. Le he pedido a cada estudiante que lleve un diario de todos los alimentos que coma y que categorice los alimentos en los grupos alimenticios básicos. De ser posible, haga comentarios sobre los alimentos que cenen y a qué grupo alimenticio pertenecen. Esto le ayudaría a _____ a tener una mejor comprensión.

We will be exploring _____ over the next few weeks. I will be asking each student to keep a diary of _____. It would be beneficial if you could remind _____ to write daily entries.

Science Fair time is just around the corner. It would be great if you could help _____ think of some ideas for his Science Fair project.

I wanted to let you know that we will be completing a science unit exploring the effects of drugs and alcohol on the human body. I think it is very important that students clearly understand the effect drugs and alcohol can have on their bodies, brains, and overall development.

Vamos a explorar _____ en las próximas semanas. Le pediré a cada estudiante que lleve un diario de_____ . Sería beneficioso que usted le recordara a _____ que escriba todos los días en su diario.

La Feria de la Ciencia va a ser muy pronto. Sería genial que usted le ayudara a _____ a pensar algunas ideas para su proyecto para la Feria de la Ciencia.

Quería informarle de que vamos a trabajar en una unidad de ciencias que explora los efectos de las drogas y el alcohol en el cuerpo humano. Creo que es muy importante que los estudiantes entiendan claramente cuáles pueden ser los efectos que el alcohol y las drogas pueden tener en sus cuerpos, en su cerebro y en su desarrollo integral.

Social Studies
Ciencias sociales

Succeeding/Improving

I am very pleased with _____ 's progress in social studies. We have been studying _____ and _____ has willingly volunteered his thoughts and participated in all the activities we have been doing.

_____ has done a wonderful job keeping the class up to date on current events. I want to thank you for the help you have given _____ and to thank him for his efforts. He has helped the entire class by bringing world events into our room.

_____ loves _____ . She seems to have a good understanding of the topic and enjoys studying it.

_____ seems to have a gift for _____ . He loves it and seems to have a real grasp of _____ . _____ is doing very well in this subject area and should be encouraged to do more outside reading in this subject.

We studied _____ this grading period, and I was pleased with _____ 's overall approach to the assignments and projects. She did very well and really put forth a great effort.

_____ puts a tremendous amount of effort into his social studies work. It appears that social studies is his favorite class. He never misses a project or assignment and is always willing to do extra credit work. It is really a joy to have _____ in social studies class.

Logros/Mejoría

Estoy muy contento(a) con el progreso de _____ en ciencias sociales. Hemos estado estudiando _____ y _____ ha compartido sus pensamientos voluntariamente y ha participado en todas las actividades .

_____ ha realizado un gran trabajo al mantener la clase al corriente de sucesos de actualidad. Quiero agradecerle la ayuda que le ha brindado a _____ y agradecerle a él/ella su esfuerzo. Ha ayudado a toda la clase al traer sucesos mundiales a nuestro salón de clases.

_____ adora _____ . Parece que entiende bien el tema y le gusta estudiarlo.

_____ parece tener talento para _____ . Le gusta y parece realmente comprender _____ . _____ va muy bien en esta materia y se le debe motivar a leer más sobre este tema.

Estudiamos _____ durante este periodo escolar, y estuve contento(a) con la actitud general de _____ con respecto a tareas y proyectos. Lo hizo muy bien y realmente se esforzó mucho.

_____ se esmera mucho en su trabajo de ciencias sociales. Parece que ciencias sociales es su clase favorita. Nunca deja de hacer ningún proyecto o tarea y siempre está dispuesto a hacer trabajo adicional. Realmente es un placer tener a _____ en la clase de ciencias sociales.

I know social studies is not _____ 's favorite subject, but _____ really enjoys _____ . I am happy to tell you that _____ has really excelled during recent weeks. Please encourage her to keep up the good work.

Sé que ciencias sociales no es la clase favorita de _____ , pero _____ realmente disfruta _____ . Me complace informarle que _____ realmente ha sobresalido en las últimas semanas. Por favor, anímelo(a) a seguir haciendo un buen trabajo.

Struggling

_____ is having a difficult time memorizing the information we are studying about _____ . I believe he is having a problem organizing the material so that he can study it. We have discussed study tips that I hope will help. It may also be helpful if you could make sure he has a quiet, neat study area at home where he can work undisturbed.

Avance con dificultades

_____ tiene dificultades para memorizar la información que estamos estudiando sobre _____ . Creo que tiene problemas para organizar el material para poder estudiarlo. Hemos repasado consejos para estudiar y espero que le ayuden. También sería útil que usted se asegurara de que tenga un área de estudio organizada y silenciosa en casa, donde pueda trabajar sin distracciones.

_____ is having a hard time with _____ . I have been giving _____ activities to help, but he seems to be having a particularly difficult time. I think that after working through some extra activities and assignments, he will do fine.

_____ tiene dificultades con _____ . Le he estado dando actividades de _____ para ayudarle, pero parece tener muchos problemas. Creo que después de que haga algunas actividades y tareas adicionales, va a salir bien.

_____ is having a difficult time with social studies. _____ seems to be a challenge for him. _____ will have to give his best effort, both in school and studying at home, if he is going to be successful in this subject.

_____ tiene dificultades con ciencias sociales. _____ parece ser un reto para él/ella. _____ va a tener que esforzarse más, tanto en la escuela como en casa, si es que desea tener éxito en esta materia.

Attitude and Behavior

I feel that _____ does not think that social studies is an important class. Her poor attitude is being reflected in the quality of her work and the inconsistency with which she is completing assignments.

Actitud y comportamiento

Creo que _____ no piensa que la clase de ciencias sociales sea importante. Su actitud se está viendo reflejada en la calidad de su trabajo y en la inconsistencia en sus trabajos.

We spent much of this grading period studying _____ . This did not appear to be _____ 's favorite subject area, and he did not seem to put forth his best effort. I have spoken with him, and he knows that I expect to see improvement.

Gran parte de este periodo escolar lo pasamos estudiando _____ . Parece que esta materia no es la favorita de _____ , y no se esforzó demasiado. Le he hablado y sabe que espero que mejore.

We have been studying _____ , and I was disappointed with the effort _____ put forth. He only participated when called upon and did only the minimum. _____ and I have discussed his performance, and he has assured me he will work harder in the future.

Hemos estado estudiando _____ , y estoy decepcionado(a) con el rendimiento de _____ . Sólo participó cuando se le pidió e hizo sólo lo mínimo. _____ y yo hemos discutido su desempeño, y me ha asegurado que va a trabajar más en el futuro.

We have been studying _____ . At the end of the unit, each student gave an oral report. _____ was very concerned about the oral presentation. She had a difficult time talking in front of the class. We will be doing more oral presentations during the year, so it might be helpful if you encourage _____ to practice several times in front of a mirror and then in front of you (in Spanish or in English) before her next presentation.

Hemos estado estudiando _____ . Al final de la unidad, cada estudiante dió un informe oral. _____ estaba muy preocupado(a) por su informe oral. Le fue muy difícil hablar frente a la clase. Haremos más presentaciones orales en el año. Usted podría ayudar motivando a _____ a practicar varias veces frente a un espejo y luego frente a usted (en español o en inglés) antes de su próxima presentación.

I am concerned that _____ is having problems in social studies class. He has a hard time taking turns and tends to interrupt others while they are talking. I will be working with him to improve these skills, and I thought it was important that you be aware of the situation. I think it would help if you would talk to _____ about what is happening.

Me preocupa que _____ tenga dificultades con la clase de ciencias sociales. Le cuesta trabajo tomar su turno y tiende a interrumpir a los demás mientras hablan. Voy a trabajar a su lado para mejorar estas destrezas, y pensé que era importante que usted estuviera consciente de la situación. Creo que sería bueno que usted hablara con _____ sobre lo que está pasando.

_____ seems to spend too much time socializing in class, rather than paying attention and learning about history. I have explained to _____ that if he is going to be successful in this class he must give it his full attention.

_____ pasa mucho tiempo socializando en clase, en vez de poner atención y aprender historia. Le he explicado a _____ que si desea lograr éxito en esta clase debe de poner toda su atención.

Informing Parents of Class Activities
Our class will be studying holidays around the world, and we are planning to celebrate several of them in the classroom. I am asking students and parents to volunteer to make decorations and cook various foods. If you wish to volunteer to decorate or cook for one of the holidays, please ask your child to let me know.

We are going to be studying _____ soon. There will be several programs about this topic on television. I will be sending home a list telling you when these programs will be on. I think it would be helpful for _____ to watch them.

Informando a los padres de familia de las actividades de la clase
Nuestra clase va a estudiar los días de fiesta alrededor del mundo y estamos planeando celebrar varios de ellos en el salón de clases. Les estoy pidiendo a los estudiantes y padres de familia que se ofrezcan como voluntarios para hacer decoraciones y cocinar varios platillos. Si usted desea participar cocinando o haciendo decoraciones para alguna de nuestras festividades, por favor pídale a su hijo(a) que me avise.

Pronto vamos a estar estudiando _____ . Habrá varios programas sobre este tema en la televisión. Voy a enviar una lista a casa para darle la información de estos programas. Creo que será bueno para _____ verlos.

Computer Skills
Habilidades computacionales

Succeeding/Improving

Computer class is clearly _____ 's favorite class. He has shown a real talent for computers. To encourage him to develop this talent to its fullest potential, I will schedule _____ for extra time in the computer lab.

_____ has excellent computer skills and really enjoys working and exploring on the computer. If you have a computer at home, you could encourage _____ to practice using it. Computers are also available for use at the local library. You may also consider enrolling her in a computer class.

Logros/Mejoría

La clase de computación es claramente la favorita de _____ . Ha demostrado gran talento con las computadoras. Para motivarlo(a) a desarrollar este talento en todo su potencial, le reservaré a _____ tiempo adicional en el laboratorio de computadoras.

_____ tiene excelentes destrezas computacionales y realmente disfruta de trabajar con la computadora y de explorarla. Si tiene computadora en casa, podría animar a _____ a practicar usándola. También hay computadoras disponibles en la biblioteca local. Además, podría considerar inscribirlo(a) en una clase de computación.

Struggling

_____ loves using the computer. He can use the Internet to find whatever information he is seeking. His typing skills, however, are weak. I will make sure _____ practices typing on the programs we have at school.

_____ has excellent typing skills, but I believe his penmanship is suffering because he tries to use the computer exclusively and almost never writes anything by hand. I will ask _____ to do about half of his written work on the computer and the other half by hand.

Avance con dificultades

A _____ le gusta usar la computadora. Puede usar la Internet para encontrar la información que esté buscando. Sin embargo, su destreza en mecanografía no es tan buena. Me aseguraré de que _____ practique con los programas que tenemos en la escuela.

_____ tiene excelentes destrezas para usar el teclado, pero creo que su caligrafía se está deteriorando porque trata de usar la computadora exclusivamente y casi nunca escribe nada a mano. Le pediré a _____ que haga más o menos la mitad de su trabajo a mano.

_____ seems to know very little about the computer. I will arrange for her to have a computer buddy at school. Her buddy will show her how to use the basic programs and how to use the Internet. If you have a computer at home, you could encourage _____ to practice using it. Computers are also available for use at the local library.

_____ seems to be intimidated by computers and is not always sure what to do. If you have access to a computer, he may benefit from spending some time on it just to help build his self-confidence. If you do not have a computer at home, they are available for use at the local library.

_____ parece saber muy poco acerca de computadoras. Haré los arreglos necesarios para que tenga un compañero de computadora en la escuela. Su compañero le mostrará cómo usar los programas básicos y la Internet. Si usted tiene una computadora en casa, podría animar a _____ a practicar usándola. También hay computadoras disponibles en la biblioteca local.

A _____ parecen intimidarle las computadoras y no siempre está seguro de qué hacer. Si usted tiene acceso a una computadora, a él/ella podría beneficiarle pasar algún tiempo usándola para ayudarle a sentirse más seguro de sí mismo. Si no tiene computadora en casa, hay unas disponibles en la biblioteca local.

Art

_____ 's scissors skills are excellent. She loves to color, cut, and paste. It is fun to watch her create. She seems to love art class.

_____ takes real pride in her artwork and seems to enjoy it.

_____ loves to draw and appears to be very talented. He is always drawing in his notebooks. You might consider getting him a sketchpad and a small set of drawing pencils to encourage his talent.

_____ seems to enjoy art class. He loves looking at pictures and talking about them. It would be beneficial if you had an opportunity to take him to an art museum.

The students have been exploring different art mediums, working with watercolors, clay, oils, charcoals, etc. _____ has shown an incredible talent for _____ . Her work is exceptional for her age and she should be encouraged to pursue her talents.

_____ loves art class and eagerly participates. Unfortunately, she never wants to help clean up at the end of class. We have discussed this and she knows that if she is going to participate she must help clean up at the end.

Arte

La destreza de _____ para usar las tijeras es excelente. Le gusta colorear, cortar y pegar. Es divertido ver cómo crea cosas. Parece que le gusta mucho la clase de arte.

_____ siente mucho orgullo de su trabajo de arte y parece disfrutarlo.

A _____ le gusta dibujar y parece tener mucho talento. Siempre está dibujando en sus cuadernos. Podría considerar darle una libreta de dibujo y un pequeño juego de lápices de dibujo para estimular su talento.

_____ parece disfrutar de la clase de arte. Le gusta ver pinturas y hablar sobre ellas. Sería beneficioso que tuviera la oportunidad de ir a un museo de arte.

Los estudiantes han estado estudiando varios medios de arte, han trabajado con acuarelas, barro, pinturas al óleo, carboncillo, etc. _____ ha demostrado un talento increíble para _____ . Su trabajo es excepcional para su edad y se le debe estimular a seguir su talento.

A _____ le encanta la clase de arte y participa con gran entusiasmo. Desafortunadamente, nunca quiere ayudar a limpiar al final de la clase. Hemos hablado de esto y sabe que si va a participar, debe ayudar a limpiar al final.

_____ 's scissors skills are not quite as strong as they should be. His fine motor skills just need to develop a little more. It may be helpful if you encourage him to cut out pictures from old magazines or newspapers at home.

La destreza de _____ para usar las tijeras no es tan buena como debiera. Sus habilidades motoras finas sólo necesitan desarrollarse un poco más. Podría ser útil que usted lo/la animara a recortar fotos de revistas o periódicos viejos en casa.

_____ seems to enjoy art but has trouble completing her projects. This has become very frustrating for her. Please encourage her to complete unfinished work at home. This should give her a better sense of accomplishment.

_____ parece disfrutar del arte, pero tiene dificultad para terminar sus proyectos. Esto ha sido muy frustrante para él/ella. Por favor, anímelo(a) a terminar trabajos inconclusos en casa. Esto debe darle una sensación de triunfo.

Music

_____ loves music class. She listens and gets involved in whatever piece of music is playing. It is a joy to watch her.

Música

A _____ le encanta la clase de música. Escucha y participa en cualquier pieza musical que se esté tocando. Es un placer verla(o).

_____ seems to have an aptitude for music and is interested in playing an instrument. He can recognize many instruments by sound, is able to read notes, and can identify simple forms of music. I would encourage him to play an instrument if he continues to be interested.

Parece que _____ tiene aptitud para la música y se interesa por tocar un instrumento. Puede reconocer el sonido de muchos instrumentos, sabe leer notas y puede identificar formas simples de música. Yo lo/la estimularía a tocar algún instrumento si continúa interesado(a).

_____ has a difficult time sitting still and listening in music class. She tends to talk to her neighbor and disrupt the class. We have talked about her behavior, and I will evaluate it over the next few weeks.

A _____ le cuesta trabajo estar quieto y escuchar música en clase. Tiende a hablar con sus compañeros e interrumpir la clase. Hemos hablado de su comportamiento, el cual evaluaré en las próximas semanas.

_____ does not seem interested in music class and often has a difficult time paying attention. We have discussed this and he seems to be trying harder, but music is not his favorite class.

A _____ parece no interesarle la música y le cuesta trabajo poner atención. Hemos hablado sobre esto y parece que está tratando de poner atención, pero música no es su clase favorita.

Physical Education
Educación física

Succeeding/Improving

_____ is not always the strongest athlete in the class, but she is always willing to participate and sets a wonderful example for the rest of the class.

_____ is always a good team member and is willing to play on any team to which he is assigned. It is a pleasure having him in class.

_____ has learned to be a great team member. She is supportive of her fellow players and is a good sport. It has been a pleasure to watch her grow and mature.

_____ is a very talented athlete. He is a born captain and a leader. He sets an excellent example for his teammates.

Physical education class has been very good for _____ this year. Her motor skills have improved dramatically. You should be very pleased with her progress.

_____ has really benefited from his physical education classes this year. He seems to understand that it is important to take turns and that he cannot always win. You should be very proud of his progress.

Logros/Mejoría

_____ no siempre es el/la más fuerte atleta de la clase, pero siempre está dispuesto(a) a participar y es un maravilloso ejemplo para el resto de la clase.

_____ siempre es un(a) buen(a) jugador(a) de equipo y está dispuesto(a) a jugar con cualquier equipo que se le asigne. Es un placer que esté en mi clase.

_____ ha aprendido a ser un(a) gran jugador(a) de equipo. Apoya a sus compañeros y tiene muy buena actitud deportiva. Ha sido un placer verlo(a) crecer y madurar.

_____ es un(a) atleta talentoso(a). Es un(a) capitán(capitana) y líder nato(a). Les pone un excelente ejemplo a sus compañeros de equipo.

Educación física ha sido una buena clase para _____ este año. Sus habilidades motoras han mejorado muchísimo. Used debe estar muy satisfecho con su progreso.

_____ realmente se ha beneficiado de las clases de educación física este año. Entiende que es importante tomar su turno y que no siempre puede ganar. Usted debe estar muy orgulloso de su progreso.

Developmental Concerns

_____ should be encouraged to participate in more outdoor activities and team sports. His _____ is a little weak and playing more outdoor games may help him develop these skills.

Behavioral Concerns

_____ would benefit from participating in a team sport on a regular basis. He has a hard time taking turns and can show poor sportsmanship. If he played on a team regularly, it might help him develop these skills.

_____ knows that suitable clothing and proper shoes are required in order to participate in gym class. Although it is his responsibility to remember them, perhaps you could help him find ways to carry out this responsibility.

_____ often chooses to wear a dress or skirt on gym days. If she wears a dress or skirt, she needs to wear shorts under it.

_____ never seems to remember to bring his gym clothes on gym day. Perhaps you could help him remember to bring them on _____ .

Preocupaciones sobre el desarrollo

A _____ se le debe animar a participar en más actividades al aire libre y deportes en equipo. Su(s) _____ es/son un poco débil(es) y jugar más al aire libre podría ayudarle a desarollar estas habilidades.

Preocupaciones sobre el comportamiento

A _____ le beneficiaría participar rutinariamente en un deporte de equipo. No sabe tomar su turno y a veces no demuestra espíritu deportivo. Si jugara en un equipo regularmente, eso podría ayudarle a desarrollar estas habilidades.

_____ sabe que se requiere ropa y calzado apropiados para participar en la clase de educación física. A pesar de que es su responsabilidad acordarse de traerlos, quizá usted pueda ayudarle a encontrar maneras de cumplir con esta responsabilidad.

_____ frecuentemente opta por vestir una falda o un vestido en los días de educación física. Si usa un vestido o una falda necesita usar shorts debajo.

_____ nunca recuerda traer su ropa de educación física en los días que tiene esta clase. Quizá usted podría ayudarle a recordar traerla los _____ .

_____ is a good athlete. She is often not happy playing on a team, however, unless she is the captain. In gym class, everyone gets a chance to be captain no matter how weak or strong an athlete she is. Please help me to encourage _____ to be more of a team player.

_____ tends to take our gym class a little too seriously. He has little patience for weaker athletes. We have emphasized that in our class we play for fun. _____ has a difficult time with this concept, as he always plays to win. You might want to discuss his feelings with him and encourage him to do his best, but to be patient with his teammates.

_____ es un(a) buen(a) atleta. A veces no le gusta jugar en equipo, a menos que él/ella sea el capitán/la capitana del equipo. En la clase de educación física, todos tienen la oportunidad de ser capitanes de equipo, no importa que tan débiles o fuertes sean. Por favor, ayúdeme a animar a _____ a ser un(a) mejor jugador(a) en equipo.

_____ tiende a tomarse la clase de educación física demasiado en serio. Tiene poca paciencia con los deportistas más débiles. Hemos enfatizado que en la clase jugamos por diversión. A _____ le cuesta trabajo entender este concepto, pues siempre juega para ganar. Quizá usted podría hablar de sus sentimientos con él/ella y animarlo(a) a hacer un buen trabajo, pero siendo paciente con sus compañeros.

Work/Study Habits
Hábitos de trabajo/Estudio

Listening/Following Directions

_____ is an excellent student capable of grasping even the most complex directions in either a written or an oral format. He is a delight to have in class and does very well in school!

_____ does quite well in her schoolwork and is a very good listener. She follows directions well and pays attention in class.

_____ could benefit from working harder on his listening skills. He is easily distracted and therefore, at times, does not listen to or follow all of the directions being given.

_____ seems to have a hard time following oral directions, especially if there are two or more directions. Perhaps working on this at home might help. Give _____ a series of directions and help him think them through. You might want to approach this as a fun game with both you and your child taking turns giving directions in Spanish or in English.

_____ is very creative but doesn't like to follow specific directions. She prefers to do assignments her own way. We have discussed this in class, and although I'm not extremely concerned at this time, I did want to make you aware of the situation.

Escuchar/Seguir instrucciones

_____ es un(a) excelente estudiante capaz de entender hasta las instrucciones más complicadas, ya sea en formato escrito u oral. Es un placer que esté en la clase ¡y va muy bien en la escuela!

_____ va muy bien en la escuela y es muy bueno(a) para escuchar. Sabe seguir instrucciones y pone atención en clase.

A _____ podría ayudarle esforzarse un poco más en su habilidad para escuchar. Se distrae fácilmente y por eso, a veces, no escucha o no sigue las instrucciones que se dan.

A _____ le cuesta trabajo seguir instrucciones orales, especialmente si hay dos o más indicaciones. Quizá le pueda ayudar trabajar en esta área en casa. Déle a _____ una serie de instrucciones y ayúdele a pensarlas. Tal vez si le plantea esto como un juego en donde él/ella y usted se turnen para dar instrucciones en español o en inglés.

_____ es muy creativo(a), pero no le gusta seguir instrucciones específicas. Prefiere hacer los trabajos a su manera. Hemos hablado de esto en clase y aunque no estoy sumamente preocupado(a) por esto en este momento, quería que usted estuviera al tanto de este asunto.

Class Work

_____ is a pleasure to have in class. She works hard and uses her time wisely to complete her class work accurately. She sets an excellent example for the other students.

_____ takes an interest in his schoolwork and is eager to participate in class activities.

_____ seems to enjoy class but never raises her hand or participates voluntarily. We have discussed this, and I have encouraged her to join in class activities and discussions.

_____ is doing a good job academically this grading period, but she needs to improve the speed with which she does most assignments. She tends to work very slowly and generally does not finish an assignment within the allotted time. We have talked about her need to push harder and try to work faster.

_____ is trying very hard in school but he rushes through assignments and tends to make careless errors. We have discussed the fact that he needs to slow down, work more carefully, and check his work before turning it in.

Homework

_____ consistently turns in complete and accurate homework assignments. He is a very responsible student.

Trabajo en clase

Es un placer tener a _____ en clase. Trabaja mucho y usa su tiempo efectivamente para terminar su trabajo adecuadamente. Es un excelente ejemplo para los demás estudiantes.

_____ se interesa en su trabajo escolar y está ansioso(a) por participar en las actividades de la clase.

_____ disfruta de la clase, pero nunca levanta la mano o participa voluntariamente. Hemos hablado de esto y lo/la he animado a unirse a las actividades y discusiones de la clase.

_____ está haciendo un buen trabajo académico en este periodo escolar, pero necesita mejorar la velocidad con la cual hace sus trabajos. Tiende a trabajar muy despacio y generalmente no termina lo que se le asigna en el tiempo dado. Hemos hablado de su necesidad de intentar trabajar más rápido.

_____ está trabajando mucho en la escuela, pero hace los trabajos escolares precipitadamente y tiende a cometer errores por falta de atención. Hemos hablado sobre el hecho de que necesita trabajar más despacio, y verificar su trabajo antes de entregarlo.

Tarea

Consistentemente, _____ entrega su tarea completa y bien hecha. Es un(a) estudiante muy responsable.

_____ is a cooperative and hard-working student. She completes all of her homework assignments and is always prepared for class discussions and tests.

Getting ready to complete assignments appears to be hard for _____ . It might be helpful if you help her make sure she is prepared with assignment information, books, paper, pencil, etc., when it is time for her to do homework. A quiet place to work at home with good lighting would also help.

_____ often forgets and leaves the books he will need to do his homework at school. I have developed an assignment sheet that requires him to list his assignments and which books he will need to complete each one. If you could review this sheet with _____ and make sure he has all of the books he will need, it may help him get organized.

It appears that _____ 's attitude toward his homework assignments seems to be shifting. It is important that he gives them his best effort. Perhaps if you review them nightly and reinforce their importance, _____ will get back on track.

_____ is easily distracted while studying. It might be helpful if you could make sure that she has a quiet place to work that is free of distractions when doing homework assignments.

_____ es un(a) estudiante que trabaja mucho y es cooperativo(a). Termina toda su tarea y siempre está preparado(a) para los exámenes y las discusiones en clase.

Para _____ , es difícil estar listo(a) para terminar trabajos escolares. Podría ser beneficioso que usted le ayudara a asegurarse de que está preparado(a) con la información del trabajo, libros, papel, lápiz, etc., cuando sea tiempo de hacer su tarea. Un lugar tranquilo, con buena iluminación, para trabajar en casa podría ayudarle.

_____ frecuentemente olvida y deja en la escuela los libros que va a necesitar para hacer su tarea. He desarrollado una hoja de tareas que requiere que haga una lista de sus tareas y de los libros que va a necesitar para cada una de ellas. Si usted pudiera revisar esta hoja con _____ y asegurarse de que tenga todos los libros que va a necesitar, esto le ayudaría a organizarse.

Parece que la actitud de _____ hacia su tarea está cambiando. Es importante que haga un buen trabajo en sus tareas. Quizá si usted se las revisara por la noche y enfatizara su importancia, él/ella podría ponerse al corriente nuevamente.

_____ se distrae fácilmente cuando estudia. Podría ser beneficioso que usted pudiera asegurarse de que tenga un lugar tranquilo para trabajar, libre de distracciones cuando haga su tarea.

_____ needs to work on developing good study habits. We are making a checklist so he has everything he needs to do his work and to work efficiently when it is time to study or do homework.

I am concerned that _____ 's poor grades are due to her incomplete homework assignments. When she does not do her homework, she is not prepared for the next day's lesson and falls behind.

Organization

_____ has excellent organizational skills. She is always ready with the proper materials and keeps her papers and work area neat and orderly.

_____ is a very responsible and organized student. He keeps track of his assignments and turns them in when they are due.

_____ has trouble keeping his desk neat. This leads to lost items and disorganized work. I will work with him to help him develop better organizational skills.

_____ needs to work on developing her organizational skills. She can seldom find anything, and she often forgets to do assignments. It might be helpful if you get _____ a student organizer or calendar in which she can write her homework assignments and keep track of her schedule.

_____ necesita trabajar mucho para desarrollar buenos hábitos de estudio. Estamos haciendo una lista para que él/ella tenga todo lo que necesite para hacer su trabajo eficientemente a la hora de hacer la tarea o estudiar.

Me preocupa que las bajas calificaciones de _____ se deban a sus tareas incompletas. Cuando no hace su tarea, no está bien preparado(a) para la lección del día siguiente y se atrasa.

Organización

_____ posee excelentes habilidades para organizarse. Siempre está listo(a) con los materiales apropiados y mantiene sus papeles y área de trabajo pulcros y organizados.

_____ es un(a) estudiante responsable y organizado(a). Se mantiene al corriente de sus tareas y entrega sus trabajos cuando se requieren.

A _____ le cuesta trabajo mantener su área de trabajo organizada. Esto trae como consecuencia objetos perdidos y trabajo desorganizado. Voy a trabajar con él/ella para ayudarle a desarrollar una mejor organización.

_____ necesita desarrollar sus destrezas organizativas. Raramente puede encontrar sus cosas, y con frecuencia olvida hacer sus trabajos. Podría ayudarle si le diera a _____ un organizador estudiantil o un calendario donde pueda escribir sus tareas y mantenerse al tanto de su horario.

Attendance/Tardiness
Succeeding/Improving

You can be very proud of _____ , as he has perfect attendance so far this year.

_____ has not missed a day of school so far this year. This has helped her progress academically. Encourage her to keep up the good work!

_____ 's attendance improved this grading period. Thank you for your efforts.

It is very encouraging that _____ 's attendance is improving. His schoolwork also seems to be showing improvement.

Concerns

_____ 's tardiness is becoming a problem. It seems to be getting worse. It is important that she make a greater effort to get to school on time.

_____ is late for school often. This seems to be affecting his work and is disruptive for the rest of the class. Please help him get to school on time.

_____ has been absent so much this grading period that it has really started to affect his schoolwork. He is falling behind in _____ .

Asistencia/Impuntualidad
Logros/Mejoría

Usted puede estar muy orgulloso de _____ , pues lleva una asistencia perfecta en lo que va del año.

_____ no ha faltado a la escuela un solo día en lo que va del año. Esto le ha ayudado a progresar académicamente. Siga motivándolo(a) para que continúe haciendo un buen trabajo.

La asistencia de _____ mejoró durante este periodo escolar. Gracias por sus esfuerzos.

Es muy alentador que la asistencia de _____ esté mejorando. Su trabajo escolar también parece estar dando muestras de mejoría.

Preocupaciones

La impuntualidad de _____ se está convirtiendo en un problema, cada vez está peor. Es importante que haga un mayor esfuerzo por llegar a la escuela a tiempo.

_____ llega tarde a la escuela frecuentemente. Esto parece estar afectando su trabajo y es perjudicial para el resto de la clase. Por favor, ayúdele a llegar puntualmente a la escuela.

_____ ha faltado tanto en este periodo, que eso ha empezado a afectar su trabajo escolar. Se está retrasando en _____ .

_____ has missed a significant amount of school. I know this could not be avoided, but I think we need to talk about how we will help _____ make the transition back to school. He has a lot of work to make up, and I want to be sure he does not get frustrated.

_____ will be missing schoolwork while you are away. I would like to suggest that she take along work so that she does not fall too far behind.

_____ ha perdido una cantidad significativa de tiempo escolar. Sé que esto no se pudo evitar, sin embargo creo que necesitamos hablar sobre cómo vamos a ayudar a _____ a hacer la transición de regreso a clases. Tiene mucho trabajo que recuperar y quiero asegurame de que no se frustrará en el proceso.

_____ va a perder trabajo escolar durante su ausencia. Me gustaría sugerirle que se lleve consigo trabajo escolar para que no se atrase mucho.

Attitude
Positive Attitude

_____ is a delight in class and has a wonderful attitude toward his schoolwork and his extracurricular activities. He always gives his best effort and keeps a positive attitude.

_____ 's positive attitude toward her work has been critical to her success. The improvement in her grades proves the importance of a good attitude and how it can positively affect a student's achievement.

_____ has a wonderful attitude toward school. It is truly a pleasure to watch him work. I am pleased that he feels hard work and a positive attitude are important parts of succeeding in school.

_____ takes great pride in her schoolwork and in her classroom jobs. She has a terrific attitude about school and learning.

Actitud
Actitud positiva

_____ es un encanto en clase y muestra una actitud muy buena hacia su trabajo escolar y sus actividades extracurriculares. Siempre hace muy buen trabajo y mantiene una actitud positiva.

La actitud positiva de _____ hacia su trabajo ha sido esencial para su éxito. La mejoría en sus calificaciones prueba la importancia de una buena actitud y como ésta puede tener una influencia positiva en el desempeño del estudiante.

_____ tiene una maravillosa actitud hacia la escuela. Es realmente un placer verlo(a) trabajar. Me complace ver que él/ella siente que el trabajo y una actitud positiva son partes importantes del éxito en la escuela.

_____ se enorgullece mucho de su trabajo escolar y de sus trabajos en el salón de clases. Muestra una actitud excelente hacia la escuela y el aprendizaje.

Needs Improvement

Although _____ has made improvements in her attitude toward others, she still needs work in this area. This is especially true in the area of sportsmanship and respect for her fellow students. We have discussed this several times and are working on strategies that may help her make better relationships with her peers.

There are times when _____ seems to know he is going to have a bad day. His attitude reflects these feelings, and it becomes difficult for him to settle down and get any work done. We have discussed this several times and are working on strategies that may help him. I would like you to be involved in this process.

Although there have been some improvements in _____ 's attitude toward her schoolwork, they have not been very consistent. Please encourage _____ to try to maintain a positive attitude toward her schoolwork.

_____ 's attitude toward school rules is of concern. He consistently disregards them and has become increasingly hostile. Please review the importance of following school rules with _____ .

Although _____ has improved his attitude toward his peers, he will continue to need our support and encouragement to make better relationships with his classmates.

Necesita mejorar

Aunque _____ ha mejorado en su actitud hacia los demás, todavía necesita mejorar en esta área. Esto es particularmente cierto en el área de espíritu deportivo y respeto para sus compañeros de clase. Hemos hablado de esto varias veces y estamos trabajando para encontrar estrategias que ayuden a mejorar sus relaciones con sus compañeros.

Hay ocasiones en que _____ parece saber que va a tener un mal día. Su actitud refleja estos sentimientos y se le dificulta tranquilizarse y terminar cualquier trabajo. Hemos hablado de esto varias veces y estamos trabajando para encontrar estrategias que puedan ayudarle. Me gustaría que usted participara en este proceso.

Aunque ha habido algunas mejoras en la actitud de _____ con respecto a su trabajo escolar, estas mejoras no han sido muy consistentes. Por favor, motive a _____ a tratar de mantener una actitud positiva con respecto a su trabajo escolar.

La actitud de _____ con respecto a las reglas de la escuela es de preocuparse. Consistentemente las desobedece y se ha estado poniendo cada vez más hostil. Por favor, repase la importancia de las reglas de la escuela con _____ .

Aunque _____ ha mejorado su actitud hacia sus compañeros, él/ella seguirá necesitando nuestro apoyo y estímulo para establecer mejores relaciones con sus compañeros.

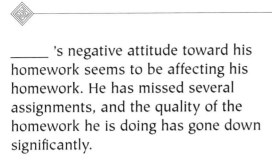

_____ 's negative attitude toward his homework seems to be affecting his homework. He has missed several assignments, and the quality of the homework he is doing has gone down significantly.

La actitud negativa de _____ hacia su tarea parece estar afectando su tarea. No ha hecho varias tareas y la calidad de las que ha entregado ha empeorado significativamente.

_____ 's report card is a reflection of her effort and attitude in school these days. To succeed she needs to improve both her effort and attitude.

La boleta de calificaciones de _____ es un reflejo de su esfuerzo y actitud en la escuela actualmente. Para salir bien, necesitará mejorar tanto su esfuerzo como su actitud.

_____ needs to improve her attitude in school. She has a difficult time accepting authority and tends to become angry if corrected. We have discussed this and are working on strategies that may help.

_____ necesita mejorar su actitud en la escuela. Le cuesta trabajo aceptar la autoridad y tiende a enojarse si se le corrige. Hemos hablado de esto y estamos trabajando en estrategias que podrían ayudar.

_____ 's attitude toward his schoolwork needs to improve if he is going to be successful this year. Encouragement and support here at school do not seem to be making as big a difference as hoped. Please encourage him at home as well. Perhaps together we can help _____ work on this.

La actitud de _____ respecto al trabajo escolar necesita mejorar, si es que quiere salir bien este año. El aliento y el apoyo que se le ha brindado en la escuela no parece tener el impacto que hubiéramos querido. Por favor, dele ánimo en casa también. Quizá juntos podamos ayudar a _____ en este asunto.

Classroom Behavior
Comportamiento
en el salón de clases

Positive Behavior

_____ 's behavior is always exemplary. He is truly a delight, and I love having him in class.

_____ has settled down this grading period. Her conduct has improved, and her academic work is showing signs of improvement.

_____ has excellent manners. He sets a great example for other students.

It is really a joy to have _____ in class. She is well behaved and has excellent manners. She sets an excellent example for her classmates.

Comportamiento positivo

El comportamiento de _____ es siempre ejemplar. Es un verdadero encanto y me gusta tenerlo(a) en clase.

_____ se ha estabilizado en este periodo escolar. Su conducta ha mejorado y su trabajo académico muestra señales de mejoría.

_____ tiene excelentes modales. Le pone el ejemplo a los otros estudiantes.

Es un placer tener a _____ en clase. Se comporta muy bien y tiene excelentes modales. Es un ejemplo excelente para sus compañeros de clase.

Noise and Disruptions

_____ has a difficult time beginning work in the morning. He is very social and would rather talk with friends than work on assignments. _____ and I have been talking about this and trying to find ways to solve the problem.

I enjoy having _____ in class. She is bright, outgoing, and lots of fun. She has a wonderful sense of humor. She has a hard time, however, working quietly. She likes making people laugh and would prefer to do that than just about anything else. I will continue to work toward having her do her tasks quietly in class.

Ruido e interrupciones

A _____ le cuesta trabajo empezar a trabajar en la mañana. Es muy sociable y preferiría platicar con sus amigos, que trabajar en lo que se asigna. _____ y yo hemos hablado sobre esto y estamos tratando de encontrar maneras de resolver este problema.

Disfruto tener a _____ en clase. Es inteligente, sociable y divertido(a). Tiene un excelente sentido del humor. Sin embargo, se le hace difícil trabajar en silencio. Le gusta hacer reír a la gente y preferiría hacer eso que cualquier otra cosa. Continuaré trabajando para que haga su trabajo en silencio.

_____ has a difficult time working quietly at his desk. He always seems to want to talk to his neighbors and often disturbs them. We have talked about his need to exercise more self-control.

Para _____ es difícil trabajar en silencio en su lugar. Parece que siempre quiere hablar con sus compañeros y frecuentemente los molesta. Hemos hablado acerca de su necesidad de controlarse mejor.

_____ had a difficult time getting back into the school routine after vacation. She tried very hard and eventually got back on track. Hopefully this will be easier after our next break.

_____ tuvo dificultades para reintegrarse a la rutina de la escuela después de las vacaciones. Se esforzó mucho y eventualmente logró ponerse al corriente. Espero que esta transición sea menos difícil después del próximo periodo vacacional.

_____ can be disruptive in class when he finishes an assignment and has free time. He needs to develop more self-control and be more responsible for himself. We have been working on some ideas that should help.

_____ puede ser un alumno problema cuando termina un trabajo y tiene tiempo libre. Necesita desarrollar un mejor control de sí mismo(a) y ser más responsable consigo mismo(a). Hemos estado pensando en algunas ideas que deben ayudarle.

_____ has difficulty making the transition from our classroom to other areas of the school. Please help me remind her to keep her hands to herself and that classroom behavior is required throughout the school and school grounds.

_____ tiene dificultad para hacer la transición de nuestro salón de clases a otras áreas de la escuela. Por favor, ayúdeme a recordarle que se porte bien y que el comportamiento en el salón de clases debe mantenerse en toda la escuela.

Not Following Class Rules

_____ often does not follow our classroom rules. We have discussed this several times. He seems to have a difficult time with self-control. He knows he still needs to try harder to follow our class rules.

No sigue las reglas de la clase

_____ desobedece frecuentemente las reglas del salón de clases. Hemos hablado de esto en varias ocasiones. Al parecer, tiene problemas para controlarse. Sabe que necesita tratar de seguir las reglas de la clase con más empeño.

I am concerned that _____ does not always conduct herself as expected in class. We have discussed her conduct many times, and I am expecting to see improvement in her behavior.

Me preocupa que _____ no siempre se comporta en clase como es debido. Hemos hablado de su conducta muchas veces y espero ver mejoras en su comportamiento.

_____ seems to have difficulty with authority. This is affecting his work as well as his relationships with other students.

_____ 's classroom behavior is inconsistent. Please remind him of the importance of following the class rules.

_____ is having trouble remembering to follow our class rules. I am sending home a copy of the rules, and it would help _____ if you would review them with him. Thank you for your help.

_____ parece tener problemas con la autoridad. Esto está afectando su trabajo y su relación con sus compañeros.

El comportamiento de _____ es inconsistente en clase. Por favor, recuérdele lo importante que es seguir las reglas de comportamiento en clase.

_____ tiene problemas para recordar que debe seguir las reglas del salón de clases. Voy a enviar una copia de las reglas del salón de clases, y ayudaría a _____ que usted revisara estas reglas con él/ella. Gracias por su ayuda.

Manners

_____ needs to work on his classroom manners. He often interrupts other students and forgets to say please and thank you. We have talked about his behavior and he understands that he needs to make a greater effort in the future.

_____ has a difficult time following our class rules, especially when it comes to being polite to other students. We have been discussing the importance of manners in general. It may be helpful if you discussed this with her at home.

_____ needs to work on his classroom manners. Whenever we have a class discussion he tends to say whatever he wants to share, without raising his hand or waiting to be called on. We are working on this in class, but it may be helpful if you discussed how important it is to let everyone share his ideas in a conversation.

Modales

_____ necesita mejorar sus modales en clase, con frecuencia interrumpe a otros estudiantes y olvida pedir permiso o dar las gracias. Hemos hablado sobre este comportamiento en clase y entiende que necesita esforzarse más en el futuro.

A _____ le cuesta trabajo seguir las reglas de la clase, en especial con lo que respecta a ser educado con los otros estudiantes. Hemos estado hablando de la importancia de los modales en general. Sería útil que usted hablara de esto en casa.

_____ necesita mejorar sus modales en el salón de clases. Cuando tenemos una discusión en clase, tiende a decir lo que desea compartir con el resto de la clase, sin levantar la mano o sin esperar su turno de hablar. Hemos estado trabajando en este asunto en clase, pero sería bueno que usted hablara de la importancia de dejar que todos expresen sus ideas en una conversación.

_____ is having a difficult time taking turns in class. We have talked about this and are working on it in school. You might also want to talk to _____ at home about how important it is to take turns.

When working in a group, _____ finds it difficult to allow other members to give their opinions. Although she often has valuable ideas, she needs to accept the contributions of others. When you are talking at home perhaps you could reinforce the need to respect the opinions of others.

_____ has a difficult time remembering his manners when working in a group. He often gets so involved and excited about what he is doing that he interrupts his fellow students and forgets to say please or thank you.

A _____ le cuesta trabajo tomar su turno en clase. Hemos hablado al respecto y estamos tratando de resolverlo en clase. Quizá sería bueno que usted le hablara a _____ en casa sobre la importancia de tomar su turno.

Al trabajar en grupo, a _____ se le hace difícil permitir que los otros miembros den sus opiniones. Aunque frecuentemente él/ella tiene valiosas ideas, necesita aceptar las contribuciones de los demás. Cuando usted esté hablando en casa, quizá podría reforzar la necesidad de respetar las opiniones de otros.

A _____ le cuesta trabajo recordar sus modales cuando trabaja en grupo. Frecuentemente se entusiasma tanto con lo que está haciendo que interrumpe a sus compañeros y olvida decir por favor o gracias.

Playground

_____ is a natural athlete and leader. It is a pleasure to watch her at play. She sets an excellent example of sportsmanship for her classmates.

_____ enjoys playing with his classmates on the playground. He plays fairly and always makes an effort to include others.

_____ 's ability to work effectively in class is often affected by problems that started on the playground. He seems to get involved in many arguments and is often not a good sport.

_____ is having difficulty practicing self-control on the playground. The other children often do not ask _____ to join in because of her temper, which tends to upset her and make her more angry. We have discussed this several times and are working to help improve her self-control.

_____ finds it very difficult to interact fairly with other students on the playground. There have been increasing incidents of poor playground behavior.

_____ is a very good student and is doing well academically. He seems very uncomfortable on the playground, however, and has a very difficult time joining in group activities.

Patio de recreo

_____ es un(a) atleta y líder nato(a). Es un placer ver cómo juega. Les pone un excelente ejemplo de espíritu deportivo a sus compañeros.

_____ disfruta de jugar con sus compañeros en el patio de recreo. Juega limpiamente y siempre hace un esfuerzo por incluir a los demás en el juego.

La habilidad de _____ para trabajar efectivamente en clase se ve afectada por problemas que comenzaron en el patio de recreo. Parece que se mete en muchas discusiones y frecuentemente no muestra buen espíritu deportivo.

A _____ le cuesta trabajo controlarse en el patio de recreo. A menudo los otros niños no quieren juntarse con _____ por su mal genio, lo cual tiende a enfadarlo(a) aún más. Hemos hablado de esto en varias ocasiones y estamos trabajando de mejorar su autocontrol.

A _____ se le dificulta interactuar con imparcialidad con otros estudiantes en el patio de recreo. Han ido aumentando los incidentes de mal comportamiento en el recreo.

_____ es un buen estudiante y va bien académicamente. Sin embargo, parece sentirse muy incómodo en el patio de recreo y tiene dificultades para unirse a las actividades de grupo.

_____ 's outside behavior causes him to be in situations in which he may be hurt. He and I have discussed this on several occasions, and he has promised to be safe. It may be helpful if you could talk with him about how important it is to follow the safety rules.

El comportamiento de _____ fuera del salón de clases lo ha puesto en situaciones en que puede resultar lastimado(a). Hemos hablado de este asunto en varias ocasiones y ha prometido tener más cuidado. Sería beneficioso que usted le hablara sobre lo importante que es seguir las reglas de seguridad.

Once _____ gets on the playground it seems he leaves his classroom manners behind. We have talked about this and are working on strategies to help him remember that good manners are expected all of the time.

Cuando _____ está en el patio de recreo, parece dejar atrás sus modales del salón de clases. Hemos hablado al respecto y estamos buscando estrategias para ayudarle a recordar que los buenos modales deben usarse siempre.

Bus/Car

_____ 's bus driver has spoken to me several times regarding _____ 's behavior on the bus. Please discuss the importance of following the rules with _____ .

Autobús/Automóvil

El conductor del autobús de _____ ha hablado conmigo en varias ocasiones sobre la conducta de _____ en el autobús. Por favor, hable de la importancia de seguir las reglas con _____ .

_____ seems to have a difficult time getting to the bus after school. He stops to talk with friends and has almost missed the bus on many occasions. We have discussed the situation several times. Perhaps you could talk to him about the problems that will arise if he misses the bus.

_____ parece tener dificultad para tomar el autobús al salir de la escuela. Se detiene a platicar con sus amigos y casi ha perdido el autobús en varias ocasiones. Hemos hablado sobre esta situación varias veces. Quizá usted podría hablarle de los problemas que podrían surgir si pierde el autobús.

_____ has left the after-school pick-up area on several occasions and almost missed his ride. _____ needs to understand that he must be responsible for himself both in school and after school.

_____ en varias ocasiones ha abandonado la parada del autobús y casi lo ha dejado ir. _____ necesita entender que debe ser responsable de sí mismo, tanto en la escuela como fuera de ella.

_____ has trouble remembering that school rules still apply even after school is dismissed. She has been in a fight while waiting for her ride home. We have talked about this, and I have explained that her after-school behavior needs to improve.

A _____ le cuesta trabajo recordar que las reglas de la escuela son válidas aún despúes de que las horas de escuela terminen. Tuvo una pelea mientras esperaba el autobús de la escuela. Hemos hablado de esto y le he explicado que su comportamiento a la salida de la escuela necesita mejorar.

Other

_____ has a difficult time settling down after recess or any other outdoor activity. She has trouble getting in line to come inside, and once she is in line, she demonstrates little self-control.

Otros

A _____ le cuesta trabajo tranquilizarse después de un receso o cualquier otra actividad al aire libre. Tiene problemas para formarse en fila para entrar y una vez que está en fila, demuestra poco autocontrol.

_____ has been having trouble being responsible when using the hall pass. He does not go directly to his destination and back. I have spoken with him about this several times, and I believe it would help if you could discuss it with him, as well.

_____ tiene dificultades para utilizar su pase de manera responsable. No va y vuelve directamente. Le he hablado de este asunto varias veces y creo que ayudaría si usted también conversara de esto con él/ella.

Character Development
Desarrollo del carácter

Responsibility

_____ takes responsibility for his actions. He exhibits terrific leadership skills and sets a wonderful example for the whole class. I truly enjoy having _____ in my class.

It is really a pleasure to have _____ in class. She sets high expectations for herself and works hard to achieve them.

It has been a joy to watch _____ grow and develop this year. He is really making good, responsible choices both in and out of the classroom.

_____ has a hard time making an independent decision and taking responsibility for it. She would rather talk to her friends and make a group decision. Putting her in various situations where she must make some independent decisions may help.

When placed in a small group situation, _____ can have difficulty accepting her share of the responsibilities. It might be helpful for _____ if she were held accountable for some specific responsibilities at home.

_____ likes to be called upon to do special class jobs, but he has a difficult time completing assigned tasks. Perhaps it would help _____ if he were given specific responsibilities at home for which he was accountable.

Responsabilidad

_____ se responsabiliza de sus acciones. Muestra magníficas dotes de liderazgo y le pone el ejemplo a toda la clase. Verdaderamente disfruto tener a _____ en mi clase.

Es realmente un placer tener a _____ en clase. Se fija metas elevadas y trabaja mucho para lograrlas.

Ha sido placentero ver a _____ crecer y desarrollarse este año. Realmente ha tomado decisiones buenas y responsibles tanto en la clase como fuera de ella.

_____ tiene dificultades para tomar decisiones independientes y asumir la responsabilidad por ellas. Prefiere charlar con sus amigos y tomar una decisión de grupo. Ponerlo(a) en situaciones donde se vea obligado(a) a tomar una decisión independiente podría ayudar.

Cuando está en un grupo pequeño, _____ tiene dificultades para aceptar su parte de responsabilidad. Sería beneficioso para _____ si se le hace responsable de algunas tareas específicas en el hogar.

A _____ le gusta que se le asigne algún trabajo especial en clase, pero se le dificulta completarlo. Quizá ayudaría si a _____ se le dieran algunas responsabilidades específicas en el hogar.

Compassion

_____ is always kind to others. He empathizes with his peers and is able to work with them in almost any situation.

_____ is a good friend and is available to support her peers.

It is a pleasure to have _____ in class. He always has something kind to say to another student who is having a bad day.

It is nice to see that _____ cares about other people's feelings. She is a kind and caring person, which she consistently demonstrates through her actions and concern for her peers.

_____ is an understanding person and is wonderful influence on his classmates. Other students often seek his advice when problems arise.

_____ has really contributed to the growth and maturity of his fellow students by continually setting a good example through both actions and words.

_____ is able to express his feelings well and demonstrates a high maturity level for his age.

_____ does not seem to realize how her actions might affect others. As you see situations occur at home, it would be helpful if you could talk about them and how they may affect others' feelings.

Compasión

_____ es siempre bueno con los demás. Simpatiza con sus compañeros y es capaz de trabajar con ellos en casi cualquier situación.

_____ es buen amigo y siempre está disponible para brindar apoyo a sus compañeros.

Es un placer tener a _____ en clase. Siempre tiene algo bueno que decirle a un estudiante que no esté teniendo un buen día.

Es bueno ver que a _____ le importan los sentimientos de otras personas. Es una persona buena y bondadosa, y lo demuestra consistentemente a través de sus acciones y su preocupación por sus compañeros.

_____ es una persona sensible y una influencia maravillosa sobre sus compañeros. Sus compañeros frecuentemente buscan su consejo cuando surgen problemas.

_____ realmente ha contribuido al crecimiento y madurez de sus compañeros, pues continuamente pone buen ejemplo tanto por sus acciones como por sus palabras.

_____ es capaz de expresar sus sentimientos de buena manera y demuestra ser muy maduro para su edad.

_____ no parece darse cuenta del efecto de sus acciones en los demás. Cuando usted vea que ocurren ciertas situaciones en casa, sería útil que usted le hablara sobre esto y cómo sus acciones afectan los sentimientos de los demás.

_____ has no problem expressing his feelings to others. Unfortunately, he often hurts other children's feelings, although he does not mean to, by speaking before he really thinks about what he says. I have discussed this with him already. Please talk to him about it at home and encourage him to consider others' feelings before he speaks.

Trustworthiness and Honesty

_____ can always be counted on to tell the truth whenever she is asked a question.

I can always trust that if _____ promises to do something, she will. This is an admirable quality.

_____ is a great friend to others. I have never seen her break the trust or confidence of another student.

_____ is popular because the other students know they can count on him and can trust his word.

I can always count on _____ to give a truthful answer to any question I may ask. I appreciate _____ 's honesty.

_____ has a real sense of right and wrong and does not let friendships sway her beliefs. She is very mature for her age.

_____ often has a hard time admitting he is wrong. He should be encouraged to be honest in all situations.

_____ no tiene problemas para expresar sus sentimientos. Desafortunadamente, a veces hiere los sentimientos de los demás, aunque no sea su intención, pues habla sin pensar realmente en lo que dice. Ya he hablado de esto con él/ella. Por favor, háblele de esto en casa y anímelo(a) a considerar los sentimientos de los demás antes de hablar.

Confiabilidad y honestidad

Siempre se puede tener confianza en que _____ dice la verdad cuando se le hace una pregunta.

Siempre puedo confiar en que _____ va a hacer lo que prometió. Esta es una cualidad admirable.

_____ es un(a) gran amigo(a) de los demás. Nunca he visto que haya traicionado la confianza de otro estudiante.

_____ es popular porque los demás estudiantes saben que pueden contar con él/ella y pueden confiar en su palabra.

Sé que siempre puedo contar con _____ para responder con la verdad a cualquier pregunta que le haga. Aprecio la honestidad de _____ .

_____ posee un verdadero sentido de lo bueno y lo malo y no deja que la amistad interfiera con sus creencias. Es muy maduro(a) para su edad.

Frecuentemente, a _____ le cuesta admitir que está equivocado(a). Debe recibir motivación para ser honesto en todas las situaciones.

_____ does not like to be wrong and sometimes has problems explaining events as they actually occurred. You might want to watch for this kind of situation at home and encourage her to be factual and truthful.

A _____ no le gusta estar equivocado(a), y a veces tiene dificultades para explicar acontecimientos tal como sucedieron. Quizá sería bueno que usted vigilara este tipo de situaciones en casa y lo/la motivara a ser objetivo y honesto.

_____ is not always truthful when asked about a situation.

_____ no siempre dice la verdad cuando se le pregunta sobre alguna situación.

It seems _____ sometimes has a problem understanding right from wrong. Please take opportunities at home to reinforce this concept.

A veces a _____ le cuesta distinguir entre lo que está bien y lo que está mal. Por favor, aproveche las oportunidades que se le presenten en casa para reforzar este concepto.

Self-Discipline

_____ shows great self-control and always strives to work out disagreements in a positive way.

Tener disciplina

_____ muestra muy buen dominio de sí mismo(a) y siempre intenta resolver desacuerdos de una manera positiva.

I am impressed by _____ 's self-discipline. He always makes sure his work is done properly before going on to a free-time activity.

Me impresiona la disciplina de _____ . Siempre se asegura de que su trabajo esté hecho adecuadamente antes de hacer algo con su tiempo libre.

You can be very proud of _____ . She sets a wonderful example for her peers and classmates.

Usted puede estar muy orgulloso de _____ . Le pone un gran ejemplo a sus compañeros.

_____ has excellent reasoning skills and applies them well in peer situations, which helps him to make good choices.

_____ posee excelentes destrezas de razonamiento y las aplica bien en situaciones con sus compañeros, lo cual le ayuda a tomar buenas decisiones.

_____ has developed good decision-making skills and is quite mature for her age.

_____ ha desarrollado buenas destrezas para tomar decisiones y es muy maduro(a) para su edad.

_____ has shown great self-discipline this year. She knows what she wants and goes after it in positive ways. It is a pleasure to have her in my class.

_____ exhibits excellent self-discipline, especially for his age. He does not jump to conclusions, but instead demonstrates excellent problem-solving skills and has the ability to take the time needed to think a problem through to its logical conclusion.

_____ is an extrovert and has many friends in the school. At times it is difficult to get her to work. _____ and I have discussed the appropriate times for socializing and working. Reinforcing this at home with her will be appreciated.

_____ has a hard time whenever there is more than one activity going on in the room. She finds it difficult to ignore the other activities and stay on task. When _____ is doing homework it may be helpful if you could remind her to stay focused and help her stay on track until the assignment is completed.

_____ can be impulsive and tends to make decisions before considering the consequences. We have discussed this several times, and over the past few weeks, _____ has really made an effort to think before making a quick a decision.

_____ ha mostrado una gran disciplina este año. Sabe lo que quiere y lo consigue de maneras positivas. Es un placer tenerlo(a) en clase.

_____ muestra excelente disciplina, especialmente para su edad. No se precipita para llegar a conclusiones, al contrario, demuestra gran habilidad para resolver problemas y tiene la capacidad de tomarse el tiempo necesario para pensar en un problema y llegar a su conclusión lógica.

_____ es extrovertido y tiene muchos amigos en la escuela. En ocasiones es difícil hacer que trabaje. _____ y yo hemos hablado acerca de los momentos apropiados para socializar y trabajar. Apreciaría que esto se reforzara en casa.

_____ tiene problemas cuando hay más de una actividad realizándose al mismo tiempo en el salón de clases. Se le dificulta ignorar las otras actividades y seguir con su trabajo. Cuando _____ esté haciendo su tarea, sería bueno que usted le recordara que debe permanecer concentrado y ayudarle a seguir con su tarea hasta terminarla.

En ocasiones, _____ puede ser impulsivo(a) y tomar decisiones antes de considerar las consecuencias. Hemos hablado de esto en varias ocasiones y en el curso de las últimas semanas, _____ ha hecho un esfuerzo real por pensar antes de tomar una decisión apresuradamente.

I have noticed that _____ tends to have a hard time staying focused and can be easily distracted from the task at hand. It would be helpful if he had a homework routine that helped him to stay focused. A study area free of distractions would also be very helpful.

He notado que a _____ le cuesta trabajo mantener su concentración y se le puede distraer fácilmente de la tarea que esté desempeñando. Sería beneficioso que estableciera una rutina para hacer su tarea que le ayudara a mantenerse concentrado. Un área de estudio libre de distracciones también le ayudaría.

_____ seems to have a difficult time being alone and working independently. She loves working in a group. She is a wonderful group member and functions well within a group. It is important, however, that she be able to work successfully on her own. I will put her in more independent situations in class, which may help.

_____ parece tener dificultades si está solo y trabaja independientemente. Le gusta trabajar en grupo. Es un maravilloso miembro de grupo y funciona bien dentro de un grupo. Sin embargo, es importante que pueda trabajar solo(a) exitosamente. Yo lo/la pondré en situaciones más independientes en clase, lo cual podría ayudar.

_____ has shown a need to be the center of attention at times. I have talked to him about being more self-disciplined in class and discussed some strategies that may help.

_____ en ocasiones ha mostrado tener la necesidad de ser el centro de atención. He hablado con él/ella sobre la disciplina en clase y hemos conversado sobre algunas estrategias que pueden ayudar.

Fairness

_____ has a terrific sense of fair play and demonstrates excellent sportsmanship.

Imparcialidad

_____ sabe jugar limpiamente y demuestra un excelente espíritu deportivo.

_____ is really an excellent sportsman and sets a wonderful example for his classmates. It is a joy to watch him play a game.

_____ es un(a) excelente deportista y les pone un marvilloso ejemplo a sus compañeros. Es un placer ver cómo juega.

_____ plays well with others and shows great maturity, even when she doesn't win.

_____ juega bien con los demás y demuestra gran madurez, aún cuando no gana.

_____ seems to really understand the importance of fairness. She takes turns and enjoys sharing with others.

Parece que _____ realmente entiende la importancia de la imparcialidad. Toma su turno y disfruta compartir con los demás.

I believe _____ needs help to develop better sportsmanship skills. He has a difficult time losing and a hard time being happy for his friends when they win.

_____ has difficulty sitting still and waiting for her turn. She is working on this problem and trying hard to remember to let everyone have a turn.

_____ has difficulty when it comes to taking turns in games. He does not have the patience to wait for his turn and often tries to take an extra turn. If you experience this behavior at home, it may be helpful if you could talk about the importance of fair play.

I am noticing that _____ has been having trouble sharing materials with others. I have talked to her about this, and she has agreed to do better. I am looking forward to seeing progress in this area.

Citizenship

I am proud of _____ . She takes her civic responsibilities very seriously and shows a desire to become more involved in community activities.

I am pleased to have _____ in my class. He consistently demonstrates a genuine understanding of other children's backgrounds. He is sensitive to cultural differences and really tries to build bridges of understanding between his classmates.

Creo que _____ necesita ayuda para desarrollar un mejor espíritu deportivo. Le cuesta trabajo perder y tiene dificultades para alegrarse cuando sus amigos ganan.

A _____ le cuesta trabajo quedarse quieto(a) y esperar su turno. Está trabajando en resolver este problema y tratando de recordar que debe dejar que todos tengan su turno.

_____ tiene problemas para tomar su turno en los juegos. No tiene paciencia para esperar su turno y frecuentemente trata de tomar un turno de más. Si usted observa este comportamiento en casa, sería de utilidad que usted le hablara de la importancia de jugar limpiamente.

He notado que _____ tiene dificultades para compartir materiales con los demás. Le he hablado de esto y ha estado de acuerdo en mejorar. Espero ver progreso en esta área.

Civismo

Estoy orgulloso(a) de _____ . Toma sus responsabilidades cívicas muy seriamente y muestra ganas de participar más en actividades comunitarias.

Me complace tener a _____ en mi clase. Consistentemente muestra una genuina comprensión del origen de otros niños. Es sensible a diferencias culturales y realmente intenta construir lazos de entendimiento entre sus compañeros.

_____ is open to learning about other cultures and beliefs. In fact, she really seems to enjoy learning about other cultures and lifestyles.

_____ is a delightful addition to our class. He respects others and follows the school rules. He sets a wonderful example of citizenship for the other students.

_____ does a great job keeping our classroom neat and orderly. She seems quite proud to be a member of our class and encourages others to feel the same.

You should be very proud of _____ . He is an excellent student and a responsible school citizen. He cares about his school and classroom and often volunteers for extra responsibilities in class.

Poor citizenship is becoming a problem for _____ . She seems to have trouble following school rules and can be disrespectful to class property.

_____ does not seem to be interested in being a part of the classroom community. Perhaps it would help if you would also encourage him to do his classroom job each day and to help the other students tidy up the room at the end of the day.

_____ está abierto a aprender sobre otras culturas y creencias. De hecho, realmente parece disfrutar de aprender sobre otras culturas y modos de vida.

_____ ha sido una excelente adición a nuestra clase. Respeta a otros y sigue las reglas de la escuela. Les pone un ejemplo maravilloso de civilidad a los demás estudiantes.

_____ hace un buen trabajo al mantener organizado nuestro salón de clase. Parece estar muy orgulloso(a) de ser miembro de nuestra clase y motiva a los demás a sentirse de la misma manera.

Usted debe estar orgulloso de _____ . Es un(a) excelente estudiante y un miembro responsable de la escuela. Su salón de clases y su escuela son importantes para él/ella, y frecuentemente se ofrece de voluntario(a) para asumir responsabilidades adicionales en clase.

La falta de civilidad se está convirtiendo en un problema para _____ . Tiene dificultades para seguir las reglas de la escuela y llega a no respetar la propiedad de la clase.

A _____ no le interesa mucho ser parte de la comunidad del salón de clases. Quizá sería útil que usted también lo/la motivara a hacer su trabajo en clase todos los días y a ayudar a otros estudiantes a ordenar el salón al final del día.

Integrity

You can be very proud of _____ . She tries to make good choices and will not compromise her integrity for others.

_____ consistently demonstrates strong, positive personal values and sets an excellent example for other students. It is a pleasure to have him in our class.

You can be proud that _____ places such a high value on personal integrity. He is very concerned about what is right and expects the same from others. He is a wonderful role model for the whole class.

Although peer pressure can be a difficult thing to resist, _____ thinks for herself and tries to make the right decision regardless of what others decide.

I am very proud of _____ . She has really matured during this school year and has been a wonderful influence on the other students. We often break into small groups to do projects, and her strong values and high level of integrity have always guided _____ 's decisions in her group.

It is wonderful to watch _____ with other students. Integrity is very important to him, and he communicates this to his fellow students in all situations.

_____ seems to be easily influenced by others. It also appears she will compromise what is important to her in order to be accepted by the group.

Integridad

Usted puede estar muy orgulloso de _____ . Trata de tomar buenas decisiones y no compromete su integridad por los demás.

Consistentemente, _____ demuestra valores personales positivos y fuertes, y da un excelente ejemplo a otros estudiantes. Es un placer que esté en nuestra clase.

Usted puede estar orgulloso, pues _____ le otorga un gran valor a la integridad personal. Le preocupa hacer lo correcto y espera lo mismo de los demás. Es un maravilloso modelo a seguir para toda la clase.

Aunque la presión de los compañeros puede ser algo difícil de resistir, _____ piensa por sí mismo(a) y trata de tomar la decisión correcta independientemente de lo que decidan los demás.

Estoy muy orgulloso(a) de _____ . Realmente ha madurado durante este año escolar y ha sido una maravillosa influencia para otros estudiantes. Frecuentemente, nos dividimos en pequeños grupos para realizar proyectos, y sus fuertes valores y alto nivel de integridad siempre han guiado las decisiones de su grupo.

Es maravilloso ver a _____ con otros estudiantes. La integridad es muy importante para él/ella y se lo comunica a sus compañeros en toda situación.

_____ puede ser influenciado(a) muy fácilmente por los demás. También parece que él/ella compromete lo que es importante para él/ella para ser aceptado(a) en el grupo.

_____ is a good student and sets high standards for himself. Recently, however, he has made some new friends, and I have seen some changes that may be of concern. It seems that when _____ is with his friends, their approval influences his decisions.

_____ is very concerned about not fitting in, and this can affect her judgement at times. She knows what is right and only needs encouragement.

_____ continues to reach for high personal and academic standards for himself and for those around him. He often seems disappointed, however, by others who fail to reach the high standards that he has set.

Perseverance

I applaud _____ 's perseverance. She is always willing to try and gives her best effort in any situation, even when she does not meet with immediate success.

It is wonderful that _____ is always willing to try and give his best effort on any project. His enthusiasm and perseverance are appreciated by all.

_____ has shown great progress this quarter. She has really persevered through some tough challenges, and her grades reflect her efforts. Her hard work has certainly paid off.

_____ es un(a) buen(a) estudiante y se fija altos estándares. Sin embargo, recientemente ha hecho nuevos amigos y he notado algunos cambios que pueden ser preocupantes. Parece que cuando _____ está con sus amigos, la aprobación de ellos influye en sus decisiones.

A _____ le preocupa mucho no congeniar con los que le rodean, y esto puede afectar su juicio en ocasiones. Sabe lo que es correcto y sólo necesita apoyo.

_____ continúa tratando de alcanzar elevados estándares académicos y personales para sí mismo y para los que le rodean. Sin embargo, a veces parece decepcionarse de que los demás no puedan alcanzar los mismos altos estándares que él/ella se ha fijado.

Perseverancia

Aplaudo la perseverancia de _____ . Siempre trata de dar lo mejor de sí mismo(a) en cualquier situación, aun cuando no encuentre el éxito inmediato.

Es maravilloso que _____ siempre trate de esforzarse en cualquier proyecto. Su entusiasmo y perseverancia son apreciados por todos.

_____ ha progresado mucho este trimestre. Realmeante ha perseverado a través de algunos retos difíciles y sus calificaciones reflejan sus esfuerzos. Su arduo trabajo ciertamente ha rendido frutos.

It appears _____ is easily defeated if not immediately successful. Hopefully some extra support in class will help. Perhaps you could offer extra encouragement at home when _____ brings home her next project.

Parece que _____ se da por vencido(a) fácilmente si no logra un éxito inmediato. Esperamos que un poco más de apoyo en clase le ayude. Quizá usted pueda ofrecerle ánimo en casa cuando _____ lleve su próximo proyecto a casa.

_____ has little patience and tends to give up if something does not work on the first try. I have been working with him on this, but I think it is going to take some time and more effort on his part.

_____ tiene poca paciencia y tiende a darse por vencido(a) si algo no funciona la primera vez. He estado trabajando con él/ella en esto, pero creo que el/ella va a tener que dedicarle tiempo y esfuerzo.

It is wonderful that _____ is always willing to try something new. Unfortunately, however, she is often willing to give up if it does not come easily.

Es maravilloso que _____ siempre está listo(a) para probar algo nuevo. Desafortunadamente, sin embargo, a veces se da por vencido(a) si eso no funciona o no sale fácilmente.

Respect

_____ has come a long way this year. He is much more respectful of the other students' feelings than he was at the beginning of the year. He has made many new friends and is progressing nicely.

Respeto

_____ ha progresado mucho este año. Es mucho más respetuoso(a) de los sentimientos de los demás estudiantes en comparación con su actitud de principio de año. Ha hecho muchos nuevos amigos y está avanzando muy bien.

_____ is always respectful of the other students in the class.

_____ siempre es respetuoso(a) de los demás estudiantes.

_____ is respectful and polite to me and other adults in the school. He also shows respect for his classmates.

_____ es respetuoso(a) y bien educado(a) conmigo y con otros adultos en la escuela. También demuestra respeto por sus compañeros.

_____ is struggling when it comes to interacting with her classmates. When frustrated or upset, she appears to show little respect for the other children's feelings.

_____ tiene dificultades cuando se trata de interactuar con sus compañeros. Cuando se frustra o se enoja, muestra poco respeto por los sentimientos de otros estudiantes.

_____ can often appear abrupt or disrespectful in a disagreement. He usually feels badly afterwards. He knows it is important to always show respect even when disagreeing. We have discussed the situation, and he has promised to work on it.

A veces _____ puede parecer brusco(a) e irrespetuoso(a) en un desacuerdo. Generalmente, se siente mal después. Sabe que siempre es importante respetar, aun cuando se esté en desacuerdo. Hemos comentado la situación y ha prometido mejorar esto.

_____ often shows little respect for other students' belongings. He borrows things without asking and sometimes returns them damaged. This is causing problems with his classmates. We have discussed this and are working on strategies that should help him.

Frecuentemente, _____ muestra poco respeto por las propiedades de otros estudiantes. Toma cosas prestadas sin pedir permiso y a veces las regresa en mal estado. Esto está causando problemas con sus compañeros. Hemos hablado de esto y estamos trabajando en estrategias que podrían ayudarle.

_____ shows little respect for school rules that she feels are not important. We have discussed that the rules are for everyone and that she is expected to follow them. It may be helpful if you could talk with her about the importance of school rules.

_____ muestra poco respeto por las reglas de la escuela pues siente que no son importantes. Hemos hablado de que las reglas son para todos y que se espera que él/ella las obedezca. Sería bueno que usted hablara con él/ella sobre la importancia de las reglas de la escuela.

Peer Relations
Relaciones con compañeros

Peer Pressure

You should be very proud of _____ .
Although he takes other people's advice
into consideration, he thinks for himself and
makes good, solid decisions.

Although peer pressure can be difficult to
resist, _____ really knows what he should be
doing and does not let the group take him too
far off track.

_____ appears not to care if he continues to
do good work. He is still doing very well, as
he is a bright child who enjoys learning. I will
closely monitor the situation to make sure he
stays on track.

When working independently, _____ has
excellent instincts and does great work. In
a group, however, she is easily influenced
by others and will allow the group to go
in a wrong direction rather than voicing
a different opinion. I will try to help her
become more comfortable in a group.

Positive Peer Relations

_____ is very mature for his age and has
made friends with many of the older students
in school. I think this has been a very positive
experience for him given his maturity level.

Presión de los compañeros

Usted debe estar muy orgulloso de _____ .
Aunque toma en cuenta los consejos de otras
personas, él/ella piensa por sí mismo(a) y
toma decisiones sólidas.

Aunque la presión de los compañeros puede
ser difícil de resistir, _____ realmente sabe lo
que debe hacer y no permite que el grupo lo
desvíe.

A _____ no le importa si continúa haciendo
un buen trabajo. Aún sigue haciendo un
buen trabajo pues es inteligente y disfruta
de aprender. Yo voy a observar de cerca
la situación para asegurarme de que se
mantenga al corriente.

Cuando _____ trabaja independientemente,
él/ella tiene instintos excelentes y hace muy
buen trabajo. En un grupo, sin embargo, se
deja influenciar fácilmente por los demás
y permitirá que el grupo tome una mala
dirección antes de expresar una opinión
diferente. Trataré de ayudarle a sentirse más
cómodo(a) en grupo.

Relaciones positivas entre compañeros

_____ es muy maduro(a) para su edad y ha
hecho amistad con muchos de los estudiantes
de más edad de la escuela. Pienso que esto
ha sido una experiencia muy positiva que le
ha dado su nivel de madurez.

It is a joy to watch _____ in class. She has made progress. She has many friends and is able to take a leadership role in group activities.

_____ is always a willing volunteer and will help anyone in need. He is well liked by his classmates and is a delight to have in class.

I have really enjoyed having _____ in my class this year. She makes friends easily and is a good friend to her classmates.

Needs Improvement

_____ is a popular, generally well-adjusted student. Recently, peer approval seems to have become very important to him. I will pay attention to the situation.

_____ is doing fine academically, but she seems to be somewhat of a loner, only interacting with other students when forced. I just wanted you to be aware of the situation so that we could both monitor it.

_____ makes friends easily and is very popular in class. Unfortunately she has a tendency to socialize when she should be working. I am working with her to improve in this area.

_____ seems to be breaking away from his old friends and trying to befriend a new, much different group of students. I will monitor the situation.

Es un placer ver a _____ en clase. Ha logrado progresar. Tiene muchos amigos y es capaz de tomar el liderazgo en actividades de grupo.

_____ siempre está dispuesto(a) a participar como voluntario(a) y ayudar a quien lo necesite. Sus compañeros lo/la aprecian y es un placer que esté en clase.

Realmente he disfrutado tener a _____ en mi clase este año. Tiene facilidad para hacer amistades y es buen(a) amigo(a) de sus compañeros.

Necesita mejorar

_____ es un(a) estudiante popular y generalmente bien ubicado(a). Recientemente, la aprobación de sus compañeros parece haberse hecho más importante para él/ella. Voy a poner atención a esta situación.

_____ va bien académicamente, pero es un poco solitario(a), sólo interactúa con otros estudiantes cuando se le obliga. Sólo quiero que usted esté consciente de la situación para que ambos observemos este asunto.

_____ hace amigos fácilmente y es muy popular en clase. Desafortunadamente, tiende a socializar cuando debería estar trabajando. Estoy trabajando con él/ella en esta área.

_____ parece estar separándose de sus antiguas amistades y tratando de hacer nuevos y muy diferentes amigos. Observaré la situación.

_____ is fairly immature for his age. Therefore, he tends to make friends with younger students as he is more comfortable with them. He has been progressing nicely this year and by the beginning of the next school year should be making friends with students his own age.

_____ es un poco inmaduro(a) para su edad. De ahí que tiende a tener amigos más jóvenes que él/ella pues se encuentra más cómodo(a) con ellos. Ha estado progresando muy bien este año y para el principio del próximo año escolar deberá hacer amigos con estudiantes de su misma edad.

_____ has been having a difficult time sharing ideas with her peers. She often appears to be afraid that her ideas will be challenged or that she might be wrong. I will continue to encourage her to participate and share her ideas in class.

_____ tiene problemas para compartir ideas con sus compañeros. Frecuentemente parece tener miedo de que sus ideas no sean aceptadas o de equivocarse. Seguiré dándole ánimos para que participe y comparta sus ideas en clase.

_____ feels it is not "cool" to be smart. He often does not give his best effort, because he really wants to fit in. I will monitor the situation. Perhaps it would help if you encourage him to be his own person.

_____ siente que ser inteligente no lo/la hace popular. Frecuentemente, no da todo lo que puede dar porque realmente quiere ser popular. Observaré la situación. Quizá ayudaría que usted lo/la animara a que sea él/ella misma.

_____ seems to be having a difficult time in class making friends with the other students.

_____ tiene dificultades para hacerse amigo de sus compañeros de clase.

It has been brought to my attention that lately _____ has become somewhat aggressive on the playground. Perhaps you could reinforce the importance of following school rules and getting along with classmates.

Se me ha hecho notar que últimamente _____ se ha puesto un poco agresivo(a) a la hora del recreo. Quizá usted podría reforzar la importancia de seguir las reglas de la escuela y de llevarse bien con los compañeros.

Personal Development
Desarrollo personal

Effort

_____ 's good grades reflect the effort she puts into her studies. She consistently strives to do her best.

_____ is a joy to have in class. He sets high standards for himself and works hard, putting forth effort to reach his goals.

_____ 's work has been quite satisfactory. She is working on grade level, but she is quite bright and I believe she is capable of doing more. I would like to give her some independent work to push her to reach her potential.

_____ could be an excellent student but she does not seem motivated to work up to her potential. Hopefully being supportive and encouraging both at home and at school will help her excel.

_____ completes all assignments and turns them in on time, but it is clear that he does not put forth his best effort unless it is something he loves. It is my hope that encouraging him to broaden his areas of interest may help.

Self-Esteem/Self-Confidence

_____ seems to really have the confidence to try new things. He is not afraid to take a risk.

Esfuerzo

Las buenas calificaciones de _____ reflejan el esfuerzo que pone en sus estudios. Constantemente trata de hacer lo mejor que puede.

Es un placer tener a _____ en clase. Se fija altos estándares para sí mismo(a), y se esfuerza por lograr sus objetivos.

El trabajo de _____ ha sido muy satisfactorio. Está trabajando al nivel de su grado escolar, pero es muy inteligente y creo que es capaz de hacer más. Me gustaría darle trabajo independiente para empujarlo(a) a alcanzar su potencial.

_____ podría llegar a ser un(a) excelente estudiante, pero no parece estar motivado(a) a trabajar a todo su potencial. Ojalá que darle ánimo y apoyo, tanto en casa como en la escuela, le ayuden a lograr la excelencia.

_____ termina todos los trabajos y los entrega a tiempo, pero es obvio que no trabaja a toda su capacidad a menos que sea algo que le guste. Espero que apoyándolo(a) a ampliar sus áreas de interés, esto mejore.

Autoestima/Confianza en sí mismo

_____ realmente parece tener confianza para intentar cosas nuevas. No tiene miedo de arriesgarse.

_____ has a very healthy sense of self-worth. She is a kind, well-adjusted child.

_____ needs time to develop better leadership skills. To help with this, I will place him in some small group situations where he must take a leadership role.

I am concerned because _____ seems to have lost a lot of weight over the last couple of months and still thinks she needs to lose more. You should be aware that she never eats her lunch.

It is of concern that _____ requires a lot of positive feedback and encouragement. He is a bright and popular student but seems to have a problem with self-esteem.

Maturity/Life Skills

It is a joy to have _____ in my class. She has been a wonderful influence on her classmates. She has wonderful curiosity and enthusiasm for learning.

_____ seems to be a little immature for his age and tends to seek attention when others are around. It is important for us not to encourage or reward this behavior.

_____ is a happy and well-adjusted child who is mature for his age. He is also doing very well. He easily grasps complex concepts and exhibits a zest for learning.

_____ tiene un sentido muy sano de autovaloración. Es un(a) niño(a) bien adaptado(a) a sus circunstancias.

_____ necesita tiempo para desarrollar mejores habilidades de liderazgo. Para ayudar en este asunto, lo(la) colocaré en situaciones con grupos pequeños donde deba asumir un papel de liderazgo.

Me preocupa que _____ parece haber bajado mucho de peso durante los últimos dos meses y todavía piensa que debe bajar más. Usted debe saber que nunca se come su almuerzo.

Me preocupa que _____ requiere de mucha retroalimentación positiva y apoyo. Es un(a) estudiante inteligente y popular, pero parece tener algún problema de autoestima.

Madurez/Destrezas para la vida

Es un placer tener a _____ en clase. Ha sido una influencia maravillosa para sus compañeros. Muestra gran curiosidad y entusiasmo por aprender.

_____ parece ser un poco inmaduro(a) para su edad y tiende a buscar atención cuando se haya rodeado(a) de otros. Es importante que no se le recompense este tipo de conducta.

_____ es un(a) niño(a) feliz y bien adaptado(a) a sus circunstancias, que es muy maduro(a) para su edad. Va muy bien. Fácilmente comprende conceptos complicados y muestra entusiasmo por aprender.

When _____ is upset, she tends to cry and is then embarrassed. As she continues to mature and become comfortable with herself, these emotional swings should stop. I wanted you to be aware that this seems to be a very difficult time for _____ .

Cuando _____ se enoja, tiende a llorar y luego se avergüenza. Estos cambios de humor terminarán a medida que madure y se sienta más cómodo(a) consigo mismo(a). Quiero que usted sepa que estos son momentos difíciles para _____ .

_____ is having a difficult time in class right now. All of his friends are a year to two younger as _____ is a little immature for his age. Hopefully time will take care of this issue, but it is problematic for him right now.

_____ ahora está pasando por una etapa difícil en la clase. Todos sus amigos son uno o dos años menores que _____ , pues es un poco inmaduro(a) para su edad. Esperemos que el tiempo se encargue de remediar esta situación, pero de momento es problemática.

Although _____ appears to be a little immature for his age in some areas, he is asking a lot of tough questions regarding sex, alcohol, and drugs.

Aunque _____ aparenta ser un poco inmaduro(a) para su edad en algunas áreas, está haciendo preguntas difíciles con respecto al sexo, al alcohol y las drogas.

Social/Communication Issues

_____ truly cares about other students and their feelings. If a child is left out of a game, she will play with him. If others appear unhappy, she will try to cheer them up. _____ really is a very special person. I am delighted to have her in my class.

Asuntos sociales/Comunicación

A _____ realmente le importan los sentimientos de sus compañeros. Si uno de los niños queda fuera de juego, él/ella jugará con ese niño(a). Si otros parecen estar tristes, intentará alegrarlos. _____ es realmente una persona muy especial. Me encanta que esté en mi clase.

It is a pleasure to have _____ in class. She gets along well with her classmates and cooperates well with others when working in a group situation.

Es un placer tener a _____ en clase. Se lleva bien con sus compañeros y coopera bien con otros cuando trabaja en grupos.

_____ is a wonderful student. He is doing well academically, and his conduct is impeccable. He seems to be very serious, though. I hope I can help him relax and enjoy school more.

_____ es un(a) estudiante maravilloso(a). Le va bien académicamente y su conducta es impecable. Pero parece que es muy serio(a). Espero poder ayudarlo(a) a relajarse y disfrutar más de la escuela.

_____ is shy at school and seems to have only a few friends. She will work in a group but only if assigned to one. Otherwise, she prefers to work independently. She would rather be by herself on the playground than play with the other children. It might be helpful if you encouraged her to become involved in an outside activity that requires group involvement.

_____ es tímido(a) y sólo tiene unos cuantos amigos. Trabaja en grupo, pero sólo si se le asigna uno. De otra manera, prefiere trabajar independientemente. Prefiere estar solo(a) en el patio de recreo que jugar con los demás. Sería bueno que lo/la animara a participar en alguna actividad al aire libre que requiera la participación de un grupo.

I wanted to make you aware that _____ tends to come to class early and wants to stay late. It appears he wants more one-on-one time with an adult.

Quisiera que usted esté enterado(a) de que _____ viene a clase temprano y quiere quedarse tarde. Parece que busca más atención personal de un adulto.

_____ has a need to tell me what other students have said or done. It creates problems for her with her classmates. We have talked about the difference between telling and tattling. Reinforcing this at home might help.

_____ siente la necesidad de decirme lo que otros estudiantes han hecho o dicho. Esto le crea problemas con sus compañeros. Hemos hablado de la diferencia entre decir lo que ha ocurrido y delatar. Reforzar esto en casa podría ayudarle.

_____ seems to have a hard time interacting with her classmates. She is quite bright and works well with everyone academically. Socially, however, she is a little immature.

A _____ le cuesta trabajo interactuar con sus compañeros. Es muy inteligente y trabaja bien con todos académicamente. Socialmente, sin embargo, es un poco inmaduro(a).

Personal Hygiene/Appearance
Our class has been working in small groups, and the other members of _____ 's group have been teasing her about her breath. It might be helpful if you check and make sure _____ brushes her teeth every morning. If she does, then you might want to talk with her dentist.

Higiene personal/Apariencia
Nuestra clase ha estado trabajando en grupos pequeños y los otros miembros del grupo de _____ le han estado haciendo bromas sobre su aliento. Le ayudaría que usted verificara y se asegurara de que _____ se cepille los dientes cada mañana. Si lo está haciendo, quizá deba consultar a su dentista.

I have noticed that _____ 's clothes are often rumpled and stained by the time he arrives at school. Maybe you could discuss this with _____ , as perhaps there is something happening before school to damage his clothing.

He notado que la ropa de _____ frecuentemente está arrugada y manchada cuando llega a la escuela. Quizá usted pueda hablar de esto con él/ella, pues tal vez algo esté pasando con su ropa antes de llegar a la escuela.

I know children can be sensitive about their appearance, but it seems that _____ does not take much pride in his appearance.

Sé que los niños son sensibles a su apariencia, pero _____ no se esmera mucho en la suya.

Performance

Struggling Students

_____ is clearly giving his best effort, but he is having a very difficult time grasping the material he is expected to learn in _____ grade.

_____ is a delightful student. Unfortunately, she is having a difficult time keeping up academically. I am concerned that _____ is really not ready for _____ grade.

_____ is socially very immature. In addition, his academic skills are still not where they should be to go into the _____ grade. I really think repeating this grade would be best for him and key to his future success.

_____ has a difficult time settling down to work in class. She has a hard time understanding written directions and often needs to have them explained. Even when she understands the directions, she often cannot complete the task.

_____ is having a difficult time in school. He is having a hard time grasping many of the basic concepts and is therefore struggling academically.

_____ always gives her best effort but struggles with almost every task. It also takes her much longer than the allotted time to finish an assignment. All of this pressure is taking a toll on _____ .

Estudiantes con dificultades

_____ claramente está esforzándose, pero le cuesta trabajo comprender el material que se supone debe aprender en _____ grado.

_____ es un(a) estudiante encantador(a). Desafortunadamente, tiene problemas para mantenerse al corriente académicamente. Me preocupa que _____ no esté listo(a) para el _____ grado.

_____ es muy inmaduro(a) socialmente. Además, sus destrezas académicas no están en el nivel que deben para pasar a _____ grado. Realmente creo que repetir este grado sería lo mejor para él/ella y esencial para su éxito en el futuro.

A _____ se le dificulta tranquilizarse para trabajar en clase. Le cuesta trabajo entender instrucciones escritas y frecuentemente necesita que se las expliquen. Aún cuando entiende las instrucciones, a menudo no termina lo que se le asigna.

A _____ le va mal en la escuela. Le cuesta trabajo comprender muchos de los conceptos básicos y por eso está batallando académicamente.

_____ siempre se esfuerza mucho, pero tiene dificultad con casi todo lo que se le asigna. También le toma mucho más tiempo del asignado para terminar un trabajo. Toda esta presión está desgastando a _____ .

_____ has really given his best effort and made some real strides in _____ . He is really struggling, however, with _____ .

_____ loves school and is a conscientious student but is struggling academically in all areas.

_____ siempre se esfuerza mucho y ha dado pasos agigantados en _____ . Sin embargo, realmente está batallando con _____ .

A _____ le gusta mucho la escuela y es un(a) estudiante concienzudo(a), pero está batallando académicamente en todas las áreas.

Nota del Maestro

Note from the Teacher

Fecha • Date _____

_____

_____

_____

_____

_____

_____

Nota del Maestra

Note from the Teacher

Fecha • Date _____

_____

_____

_____

_____

_____

_____

Parent Communication Log

Student's Full Name _____

Nickname (if any) _____

Food Allergies (please list) _____

Father's Name	**Mother's Name**
Does parent speak any English? _____	Does parent speak any English? _____
Does anyone in home speak English? If so, who	Does anyone in home speak English? If so, who
_____	_____
Address _____	Address _____
_____	_____
_____	_____
Phone (Daytime) _____	Phone (Daytime) _____
Phone (Evening) _____	Phone (Evening) _____
Phone (Cell) _____	Phone (Cell) _____
E-mail _____	E-mail _____
Fax _____	Fax _____

Student's Name	Date	Form of Communication	Comments	Follow-Up